Mollie!
Jo
MW00623753

PERMISSION

TO

ROAR

for

FEMALE THOUGHT LEADERS
READY TO WRITE THEIR BOOK

MARNI FREEDMAN, M.S. LMFT

PUBLISHING

Published by MCM Publishing
9880 Shadow Road
San Diego, CA 91941
www.mcmpublishing.com

Copyright © 2018 Marni Freedman
All rights reserved.

No part of this publication may be reproduced, stored in or introduced into
a retrieval system, or transmitted, in any form, or by any means (electronic,
mechanical, photocopying, recording, or otherwise), without the prior
permission of the publisher. Requests for permission should be directed to
info@monkeycmedia.com.

Editors: Tracy J. Jones, Carlos de los Rios & Erin Willard
Book cover design by Gwyn Snider
Interior design by Monkey C Media, www.monkeyCmedia.com
Illustrations by Lori Mitchell
Telescope Image: 123RF Stock Photo https://www.123rf.com/profile_puruan

First Edition
Printed in the United States of America

ISBN (paperback): 978-0-9974413-8-3
ISBN (eBook): 978-0-9974413-9-0

Library of Congress Control Number: 2018909444

PRAISE FOR MARNI FREEDMAN'S *PERMISSION TO ROAR*

"*Permission to Roar* goes right to the heart of a problematic matter for women writers. We struggle to own our expertise, we don't feel worthy of sharing our work, we deal with imposter syndrome, we are constantly under attack from our inner critic—and sometimes our outer critics too. Enter Marni Freedman who's doling out dose after dose of encouragement and hands-on ideas and strategies for all of us to get over all that! So needed. So inspiring. Just right for women writers at any stage of their writing process."

—Brooke Warner, publisher of She Writes Press
and author of *Green-Light Your Book*

"Marni Freedman, master coach, beloved teacher, and good witch of writing has done it again! *PERMISSION TO ROAR* is a down-to-earth, thoroughly detailed, comprehensive collection of information, guidance, and inspiration—everything a writer needs to start (and finish) her nonfiction book. Thought Leaders: Take a deep breath, open it up and get to work!"

—Judy Reeves, author of *Wild Women, Wild Voices*

"You don't have to be a 'writer' to write a life-changing book. Let Marni wed her strength to your vision. You will not be disappointed."

—John Vorhaus, author of *The Comic Toolbox: How to Be Funny Even If You're Not*

"If you have ideas and a dream to write a book, but can't imagine yourself doing it, Marni Freedman's *Permission to Roar* is for you. It's a confidence-inspiring mother lode of inspiration and practical know-how that will take you from the dream to the reality."

—Judy A. Bernstein, author of *They Poured Fire on Us From the Sky* and *Disturbed In Their Nests*

"Marni is the empirical definition of the word coach. And she is a master coach to boot. For those who want a champion as you take the blindingly overwhelming, but life-giving risk to give voice to your innate wisdom, please know Marni wrote this book specifically so you could do just that! *Permission to Roar* is lightning in a bottle, brilliantly written to light your way."

—Lois Sunrich, founding director of StoryArts

"Marni is a Master Gardener. Around her, she notices what might otherwise be overlooked: seeds of pure female potential."

—Mariah McKenzie, author of *More: Journey to Mystical Union Through the Sacred and the Profane*

"Marni's coaching is bold, informed, and inspiring. Reading this book is like having your own personal writing coach who knows exactly when to support your baby steps, and yet is not shy when you need someone to kick your ass."

—KamalaDevi McClure, author of five books, including *Secret Lives of Sex Shamans*

"Inspiring, energizing, and empowering, Marni Freedman's *Permission to Roar* is just the book women need to get the ball rolling on their book! I love it."

—Elise Capron, literary agent

"*Permission to Roar* is a mammoth of a book—engaging, practical, accessible, and most of all, inspiring. If you've ever wanted to write and are feeling unworthy or lacking trust in your abilities, or that you have nothing special to offer, read this book, now! Open to any page and just start reading. You will feel confident, uplifted, and ready to roar. What Freedman has created is monumental, tender, and fierce in all the right places."

—Cherie Kephart, award-winning author of
A Few Minor Adjustments: A Memoir of Healing
and *The Healing 100: A Practical Guide to
Transforming Your Body, Mind, and Spirit*

"One of the biggest hurdles as a writer and thought leader is to have confidence that what you have to offer the world is worth sharing. *Permission to Roar* is a motivational guidebook that holds your hand throughout the writing process and will encourage you to ROAR your message!"

—Lannette Cornell Bloom, author of
Memories in Dragonflies, Simple Lessons for Mindful Dying
and founder of SimpleJoys.com

"Marni Freedman gives women thought leaders so much more than just permission to roar. She inspires them to share their message because it is a critical part of the conversation about power, leadership, and gender. Marni provides step-by-step instructions and wisdom gained from decades of experience helping shape the stories of some of today's most influential leaders. Marni is a lioness of a teacher and coach!"

—Jen Coburn, bestselling author of six novels,
including *We'll Always Have Paris*

*Dedicated to the woman who
doesn't yet believe in herself.
I see you. Let's do this.*

INTRODUCTION

I'm going to be blunt and open this book with a plea. We need your voice. And we need it now.

Women are kick-ass brilliant. I see it every day. Women study the world, interpret the patterns, notice the nuances, and illuminate the darkness. Women work hard, live fiercely, feel the trends, dive into their creativity, and share their vulnerabilities. Women create solutions, find unique alternatives and, in effect, change their communities and workplaces. How do I know all this? Because I spend hours and hours talking to women about their ideas, their hopes for our society, their views on business, medicine, science, psychology, academics, parenting, conflict resolution, relationships, healing, and exploring the world. And what I hear floors me, makes me think, and pushes me to live every day on the cutting edge of life.

But for all their talent, women often share one missing ingredient. And that ingredient is trust. Trust that what they have to say is valuable, worthy, or wanted. If you opened this book, chances are you may be wondering if you have something important to say, if anyone will care, or if you should take the time and energy to get all those amazing thoughts down on to paper.

To me, the answer is simple. Don't overthink this one. We need you, and we need you now. We need you to help shape the conversation for our current society and for generations to come. We need your ideas to challenge our current thinking, heal our spirits, and shake up our outdated ways of doing business. Think about your favorite book written by a female author. Really think about that author. What if she hadn't trusted that small inner voice that whispered, *maybe, I should write a book.* If she hadn't persevered, she would not have made an impact on your life. And guess what? Somewhere, out there right now, is a person who truly needs to read your book.

I'm not saying that writing your book is going to be easy. But I can promise you two things. One, I will be here with you. I will walk you through the process with gentle nudging, goofball stories, and as much clarity as possible. Two, writing your book may be the most important and fulfilling experience of your life.

For too long, women have taken a back seat and doubted their brilliance.

It's time to drive and shine.

HAVE YOU EVER WONDERED?

If there was a way to tap into the magic of YOU and get that on the page?

How to organize your ideas into a thought-provoking book that people can't put down?

If writing a book about your area of expertise might be the dynamic push your career needs?

If you answered yes to any of these, join me, your master writing coach and a general good witch of writing, on the journey to unlock the book that is inside of you.

I will guide you step-by-step through the writer-tested-and-approved Three-Key Method.

The Three-Key Method Will Walk You Through All the Steps of Writing

- from a kernel of an idea,
- to brainstorming and honing,
- to choosing a template and creating your outline (then connecting to and radiating your own kind of brilliance).

But wait, there's more!

Also included: countless tools to help you execute your vision, define your audience, synthesize and present your most powerful ideas, and uncover your unique writer's voice. (I tried to count the tools; I'm telling you, countless!)

And just in case you were wondering:

You are worthy.

No one is ever fully ready, but

We need your voice NOW.

WHY ME? WHY THIS BOOK?

I have been in and around the writing business for about (gasp!) twenty-six years. I have worked on all sides of the game. I have been a screenwriter, playwright, ghostwriter, editor, script and book doctor, writing instructor, and general book Sherpa. I even spent ten minutes as an agent. (Not my favorite.) I have taught thousands of writers in workshops, classes, lectures, writing conferences and retreats, and individual sessions. Every day, I teach writers how to identify their strongest material, organize it, and express it with power and poignancy.

I'm also a licensed therapist and have learned how to help writers to find their confidence, trust their voice, and unlock the magic that they often bury deep inside. I tell you all this because I want you to know that I've got you. You are not alone on this wacky writing journey. I know the landscape, the waters, the peaks and the valleys, along with the false traps and common pitfalls. Moreover, I know the tenacity it takes to get to the finish line.

On a practical level, many hours have been spent with female writers dreaming, scheming, organizing, editing, massaging, and polishing their works of art. I have learned shortcuts and found ways of asking questions that have helped the writers to execute their authentic message.

It was out of this experience that this book was born.

I hope you eat it up with a spoon.

CONTENTS

CONTENTS

Ready to get moving?

Great. But first, I'm going to tell you a little story about s'mores.

Why Aren't You Eating S'mores With the Other Kids?

I was sixteen and a junior counselor at a Jewish sleep away camp. It was late at night; the sky was bright with stars when a kind rabbi found me wandering in the woods, thinking about life. My parents were in the middle of a seriously bad (like the worst) divorce, and I didn't get how all the pieces of my life would ever fit back together again. In the near distance, we could hear the other counselors laughing and roasting marshmallows around a campfire. The rabbi and I talked about my young existential crisis a bit, and then he just looked at me and said, "Maybe, you know, try *not* thinking so much. Maybe you should just join everyone at the campfire. They're eating s'mores, y'know."

He made a good point. Never one to turn down chocolate, I nodded and began to head down to the campfire. Then I turned around and said, "Rabbi, why do you think I think so much?"

He shrugged his shoulders. "Old soul maybe, but truly, Marni, you need to lighten up. Less thinking, more s'mores. You're sixteen."

When I got to the campfire, I ate the damn s'mores and even sang a few songs. Yet, by the end of the night, I ended up talking to the oldest counselor about his struggles in graduate school, his broken engagement and, well, the very nature of existence. I will never forget the rabbi walking past the campfire, looking at me in yet another analytical conversation and just shaking his head and laughing. I could almost hear him saying, *what is wrong with that girl?*

At the end of the summer, in front of the bus, when the rabbi and I parted ways, I said, "Don't worry, I ate a lot of s'mores." But what he said next not only surprised me; it changed my life.

"I think I was wrong," he said. "A lot of people are the s'more eaters. Not many are the thinkers. You go dream and think. Then, write it all down."

I wish I could remember the rabbi's name. Because that permission to go forth and be the wild dreamer and crazy analytical thinker that I am, probably saved my life, and helped me launch my career.

From that point forward, I have been a creative thinker, a screenwriter, a therapist for foster youth, an editor, an author, a speaker, and my favorite job of all, a writing coach.

I love ideas. Big ideas, small ideas. Wacky ideas. And I love the people that have ideas and want to be part of the collective conversation. If you are anything like me, you are drawn to be part of the conversation. To listen to what is going on in the world, then to delicately add your thoughts, or sometimes shout from the rooftops. And it is my deepest hope that this book will help you to think through your thoughts, to test them, kick them around, then smooth them out until they are bright and shiny and ready for the world at large.

So here is my advice to you:

Go dream and think.
And dream some more.
Then, write it all down.

PART ONE

PREPARE FOR SUCCESS

CHAPTER 1

THOUGHT LEADERS

Nothing can be done without hope and confidence.

—Helen Keller

What Is a Thought Leader?

The term for the big, bold thinkers in society has often changed. At times, we have called them wise men and women, philosophers, conduits, or creative thinkers. Thought leaders have always existed, whether they spoke their wisdom to the tribe or wrote it down for future generations.

As part of my exploration for this book, I studied the writings of women from different generations (going back hundreds of years) and from all walks of life. What I found is that these thought leaders were watching and witnessing history, as well as tapping into a deep, inner well of wisdom. Sometimes that wisdom spoke to them in a still, small voice and other times, it showed up as a roar.

Whether it was loud or soft, each thought leader followed an intuitive call or a gut feeling, not knowing where it might lead. Then, for whatever reason, maybe because they could no longer ignore it, they paid attention to that inner wisdom and, finally, gave it a voice.

Right about now, you may be wondering, but Marni, *am I* really a thought leader? Or can I be?

My answer to you is, take a moment with me, right here and right now, to own that title. You picked up this book, the one called, *Permission to Roar*, for a reason. And that reason is that you, like many before you, have something inside that must be expressed. Some part of you wants to roar.

That's the part I'm speaking to. The part that dreams, and thinks, and yearns, and knows; she is born to create miracles. That part of you is timeless. That part of you knows no fear. That part of you can heal, and shape, and positively change our world with your gifts. That part wonders if it's time to follow that intuitive call. My job is to help you to hear the word **YES.**

Yes, YOU.

Yes, NOW.

If you can't quite see all that in yourself yet, that's okay. Keep reading, keep dreaming, and borrow my faith in you for just a bit. Soon, you will find that a few seeds of excitement can grow into fierce branches of confidence. Trust me, the more you walk down this path, the more you will be able to own the magic that only you can do.

We Come in All Shapes and Sizes

Today, as I look around me, I see female thought leaders sparking new conversations on a wide variety of topics. I see bloggers guiding the conversation about the realities (by that, I mean the joys and insanity) of motherhood. I see women discussing and inspiring one another on how to jump into politics and run for office. I am fascinated by women speaking out on everything from spirituality and body acceptance to entrepreneurship. And we need it all.

In my career, I have worked with a stay-at-home mom who figured out a unique way to create a surprising village of support so that she didn't have to do it all, all the time. I have also worked with a working mom who found a way to tackle her self-esteem and eating-disorder issues through her unique connection with horses. I have worked with an inventive therapist who is using the latest in neuroscience to help her clients tackle their issues with anger. I have worked with a mom of a young adult son with autism, writing to change how the world sees and includes special-needs adults. I have worked with survivors of rape, molestation, natural disasters, racism, mental illness, and career collapses. Each woman's experience, combined with her unique inner wisdom, brought her to the place where she was ready to grab a pen and write her heart out.

If you are a designer or a researcher, a therapist or a teacher, a workout queen or a scientist, a writer, an actor, or a crafting goddess, a poet or a nurse, a mom of a special-needs kid, a pastor or a survivor, you too are a thought leader. If you have walked through something harrowing, engaged in deep self-exploration, and learned how to not only survive but thrive, then, yes, you are a thought leader.

A Thought Leader Tends to Be

→ a person who has lived deeply and engaged in life, and who is willing to share her insights

→ a person who engages in cutting-edge thinking

→ a person who can synthesize complex information into understandable, bite-sized pieces

→ a person who has expertise born out of years of dedication toward a specific subject or unique personal experience

→ a person who has challenged the norms after living through a difficult life issue

→ a person who is a sought-after authority in her field

→ a person who is open to sharing how she tackles challenges and faces vulnerabilities, and who creates unique opportunities

→ a person who is a speaker, writer, or community organizer

→ a person who is an introvert—the quiet, never-noticed one in the back of the room who comes up with the strategies (that the loud ones in the room often take credit for)

→ a person who is an extrovert—the more outspoken and sought out, sometimes paid and rewarded for her thinking.

You May Have Noticed

Some thought leaders are recognized. Some are not. Some thought leaders are incredibly shy introverts, but that doesn't make their ideas any less brilliant. If you fit into this category, take heart. You can find a voice through writing.

I see thought leaders almost everywhere there is room for innovation and opportunities for forward-moving thinking. Let's look a little bit further into elements that you must bring to the table (you got this), and other elements that can be learned (you got this too).

What You Must Bring to the Table

- You have experience and passion for a certain topic, concept, or issue.
- You have something to add to the conversation that is unique and different.
- You are ready to listen to your inner wisdom, to give it a voice.

A SMIDGE OF HISTORY ABOUT THE TERM "THOUGHT LEADER"

Brief Timeline of the Phrase

1876 – First used as a term to describe Ralph Waldo Emerson.

1887 – *Oxford English Dictionary* offers the first citation of the phrase when describing Henry Ward Beecher as "one of the great thought leaders in America."

1990 – In the *Wall Street Journal*, Patrick Reilly refers to magazines as "thought leader publications."

1994 – Attributed to Joel Kurtzman, the first editor of the magazine, *strategy+business*. His goal was to conceptualize strategic thinking for business. He ushered in a new era of thinking about the term when he said, "A thought leader is recognized by peers, customers and industry experts as someone who deeply understands the business they are in, the needs of their customers and the broader marketplace in which they operate. They have distinctively original ideas, unique points of view, and new insights."

Urban Dictionary definition: one who influences the outcome of an organization's decisions, policies, culture, and mission.

Cambridge Dictionary definition: an expert on a particular subject whose ideas and opinions influence other people, especially in business.

What Can Be Learned

- You can learn how to synthesize complex information.
- You can learn how to impart that synthesized information to the public at large.
- You can learn how to become more of a public persona (how to speak, present, and organize a community).
- You can learn how to write.

So, to sum it up, no matter how you define a thought leader, there is one thing everyone can agree on. Thought leaders have something to say, and a desire to move the conversation forward.

What is it that you have to say?

Meeting the "Yet Lady"

My husband, ten-year-old son, and I were in Washington, DC, for the first Women's March. We were strolling along the National Mall when we bumped into the "Yet Lady." With wild golden hair and a sparkle in her eyes, the Yet Lady was a wonderfully chatty English teacher from the Midwest who casually asked my son if he liked to read. She had no idea that that particular question was not an easy one for our family. I cringed. But my son casually explained that he struggled with reading because he has severe dyslexia. He finished with, "So, I wouldn't consider myself a great reader."

The teacher got down to his level—eyeball to eyeball—and she said, "I want to teach you the most important word in the English language. I'm an English teacher, so I know."

My son's eyes got wide. "What? What's the word?"

"The word is *yet*. Maybe you're not the greatest reader—yet. For a long time, I wanted to be a great teacher, but the truth was, I wasn't the greatest teacher—*yet*. I needed more time to brew. It's okay to take your time. Just never end a *can't* sentence without adding the *yet* at the end. Okay?"

My son smiled. She had opened a door for all of us.

Next, I am going to ask you to assess your current skill set. Remember that if you find yourself traveling down the "I can't" road, you must finish your sentence with "yet."

Skill Sets That Thought Leaders Often Need

Take a moment to assess your skill set. Place a checkmark next to the areas where you feel confident

- Big Thinking
- Creativity
- Authenticity
- Understanding the Current Landscape
- A Willingness to Be Vulnerable
- Defining
- Writing
- Teaching
- Connecting Ideas
- Researching
- Synthesizing
- Critical Analysis
- Objectivity
- Creating Curriculum/Workshops
- Focus
- Social Media/Platform Building
- Storytelling
- Understanding of the Human Condition/Empathy
- Communicating Your Message
  - Speaking for small groups/workshops
  - Speaking for large groups

After you have taken a moment to look over your current skill sets (which ones you have in your toolbox and which ones you may want to work on), know that you don't have to conquer it all at once, and you don't have to do it all alone.

Essential Partnerships

You might be a natural researcher but not be the best at writing it all down. You may embrace public speaking but have no idea how to utilize social media. So, once you assess your skills, you have a choice. Decide to learn the skill sets that you currently lack, or find a partner (or partners) that have that particular skill set. Teaming up can be mutually beneficial and incredibly powerful for all. Remember that the recipe for success is the one recipe that works for you.

Hey, Marni, What If?

Q: What If I Have an Area of Expertise, But I Haven't yet Shared My Knowledge?

A: In this case, you are probably a thought leader in the making. Some people have a vast breadth of knowledge but have never shared their ideas. Often, writing a book is their first movement toward sharing their expertise.

Q: What If I Have Great Ideas, yet I Struggle With Self-Esteem, and It Keeps Me From Getting My Ideas Down on Paper?

A: Self-esteem is malleable. It is not a fixed state of being. Meaning, you can work on it. Some practical and effective approaches to increasing self-esteem are cognitive behavioral work, hypnosis, visualization, and affirmations.

How to Kick-start Your Self-esteem Boost

1. Keep your focus only on yourself. No comparing yourself to others.
2. Let go of the notion that you must do things perfectly.
3. No beating yourself up when you make mistakes, as mistakes are part of the learning process.
4. Break tasks up into bite-size pieces. When you complete a task, reward yourself.
5. Focus your mind on the things you can control.
6. Expand excitement. If it excites you, jump into it.

Q: What If I Don't Feel Confident Enough to Start the Process?

A: As you might have guessed, that's no small question. And let me assure you, you are not alone. Collectively, we tend to struggle mightily when it comes to believing in who we can be.

To dive further into this important question, I'm going to take you on a brief tour of **who we are now, where we have been, and where we can go together.**

Who We Are Now

An Unfair Generalization

I'm going to make a gross and unfair generalization. Are you ready?

Men have no trouble owning and touting their expertise. Women? Not so much.

This is not a statement pulled from research. And yes, it is a gross generalization.

But damn it if I don't find this pattern to be true much of the time.

Working with thousands of writers, here are the two trends I have noticed:

TREND ONE: A man with little-to-no schooling, training, or significant time in an industry would easily tell me that he wanted to write a book because he had a dream, or he had a big idea that worked for him once, or because, *why not? Everyone should write a book, right?* The men didn't struggle as much with self-doubt. They didn't wonder if maybe they should get more experience or learn from the other thought leaders in the arena. In general, whether the man was qualified or not, he approached writing a book with calm, cool confidence.

TREND TWO: A woman with serious accomplishments, credentials, and time invested in an industry would tell me she wanted to write a book, but she wondered if anyone would care what she had to say. Some women feared being judged, or they questioned if they were clever enough to be a writer. I found I would often spend a good month simply helping the woman to trust her ideas and abilities before we could get to the meat of the writing. In general, highly qualified women approached writing a book with tremendous self-doubt.

When I noticed these gender-based tendencies, I was taken aback. Why were the men so sure of themselves? Why did the women feel nervous about owning their knowledge or about standing out, speaking up, or claiming their big ideas as important?

To help answer that question, I voraciously read books by women who discussed this gender issue. Over time, I learned that women, while brilliant, did not own their brilliance. They were not asking for raises or even raising their hands in some cases. Women, in short, were underselling themselves.

The truth is, like most women, I didn't know my value, and even if I had, I wouldn't have known how to get it.

—Mika Brzezinski, author of
*Knowing Your Value: Women, Money, and
Getting What You're Worth*

Next, I studied the general landscape for women in the workplace. Just where did women stand? What I found out was a troubling snapshot. Currently, in almost every industry in the United States, women are underrepresented. We are underrepresented in politics, in the boardroom, on Wall Street, and in creative leadership. No big shock there, yet the numbers still hit me in the gut. Let's start with the first statistic. According to the Center for American Progress, women make up a majority of the population in the United States (about 50.8 %).

Here's What Else I Learned (as of this writing)

Women earn degrees!

- Women earn 48% of medical degrees, 53% of law degrees, 44% of master's degrees in business, 60% of all master's degrees, and 52% of all doctoral degrees.

Women work!

- Women are currently 47% of the labor force in the US and 59% of the entry-level, college-educated workforce.
- Women own close to ten million businesses, accounting for $1.4 trillion in receipts.

Women spend!

- Women control approximately 80% of consumer spending in the US.

So, if we are educated and hardworking and we often control the purse strings, WHY IS IT that women

- are only 8% of top earners, 5% of Fortune 500 CEOs, and only 14% of all executive officers
- are only 17% of Fortune 500 board-seat holders
- are 78% of the labor force in health care and social services, but are only 15% of the top execs, and only 12% of board directors
- are only 15% of the equity partners in the legal field
- are only 16% of medical school deans
- hold only 9% of IT management positions and 14% of senior management at Silicon Valley startups
- only make up approximately 3% of creative directors in the advertising field
- are only 16% of all the directors, producers, writers, executive producers, cinematographers, and editors who worked on the 250 top-earning films in the last few years?

An important side note: Did you know that when women are in positions of power, they consistently hire more women? For example, in cinema, films written or directed by women consistently feature a higher percentage of female characters with speaking roles.

Wider Gap for Women of Color

When we look at women of color, the situation is even bleaker. Currently, women of color are 36% of our nation's female population and approximately 18% of the entire US population. But women of color occupy only 12% of managerial and professional positions. Women of color hold only 3% of the board seats of Fortune 500 companies. And frustratingly, more than two-thirds of Fortune 500 companies have no women of color as board directors at all.

I knew the leadership situation for women was bad, but I didn't know it was *that* bad until I did the research, interviewed women in businesses, and binge-watched an endless stream of TED Talks. My experience plus my research showed that women are accomplished, hardworking, brilliant, creative, and cutting edge. So why aren't more women leaders yet? Why is there so much brilliance being left on the table?

What's Stopping Us?

On the one hand, I have noticed that some thought leaders tend to be people who simply won't be stopped. They have a vision, and they are going to share it, no matter the consequences. On the other hand, some female would-be thought leaders see the patterns or the writing on the wall, and they have the expertise or the reputation, but they are shyer or not used to standing in the spotlight. They are afraid of putting themselves out in front of the pack and saying, "Look over here; this is a new way of seeing things." Stepping out on the leadership ledge can be scary.

I Did an Informal Poll of Said Brilliant Women and Heard These Common Threads

- It's just plain scary.
- The path is not clear.
- There are biases and discrimination.
- It simply hasn't occurred to us to lead.
- It's not "ladylike" to stand out too much.
- There is a lack of support from friends or family.
- We have lots of demands (children, parents, health, career) pulling us in many directions.
- Speaking historically, we have only had "voices" in the last century. It was a little over one hundred years ago that we were given the right to vote. Progress is slow.

When you step up to write your book, you will most likely encounter fear, shame, panic, anxiety, or a sensation to retreat. You may hear a tiny voice inside your head say,

"Who am I to write a book?"

Or:

"Who will want to read what I have to say?"

Having these thoughts is 100% normal. By the way, all writers experience this kind of doubt; it's not just you.

The Napkin

I had just graduated USC with a film writing degree. Yeah, a film writing degree. Needless to say, there weren't a lot of people waiting in line to hire me. I was heavily in debt, and a bit dumbfounded. I wanted to produce a play I had written, yet I suddenly found myself paralyzed. I wanted to approach a director that I felt would be perfect to make the piece happen, but I was terrified. All the usual voices of self-doubt crept in. *Who am I to write a play? Who will care what I have to say?* But the thoughts that paralyzed me the most were: *What if people judge me harshly? What if my career ends before it begins?*

My mother took me out to lunch, and I shared my fears with her ad nauseam. She didn't say much. This is a woman who usually has a lot to say, but at this lunch, she just sat and listened. Then, at the end of the lunch, she wrote a quote from writer Elbert Hubbard on a napkin and pushed it over to me. It said,

> *Want to avoid being criticized?*
> *Do nothing, say nothing, be nothing.*

I nodded and put the napkin in my pocket. We didn't talk about it further until we were exiting the restaurant. She opened the door, the sunshine fell on us, and she tossed off, "I mean at some point, you gotta tell the world you're here."

I submitted the play to the director the very next day.

What my mom had taught me, but we hadn't yet labeled, was the lesson of "declaring." It was a lesson I would need to learn many times before it sunk in.

Where We Have Been

A Ridiculously Short History Lesson on DECLARING

In 1848, women were considered the property of men. Not only could we not vote, but we didn't have the right to own property, and we had no custody rights over our children. If we were beaten or abused by our husbands, it was considered what was appropriate for the man to do to keep his woman in line. The now-famous suffragist Elizabeth Cady Stanton stood up at a conference in Seneca, New York, and declared that women should be included in the Declaration of Independence. She rewrote the famous line to read, "all men AND WOMEN are created equal." This, at the time, was not a popular point of view. It was risky. She was seen as out of touch, provocative, and pushy.

Though it was not a popular move, other women took up the cause. Women like Susan B. Anthony, Sojourner Truth, Ida B. Wells, and Alice Paul (there are more; I encourage you to dive into this part of history). And a short seventy-two years later, women got the vote. This time period is often referred to as the first wave of the women's movement. It focused heavily on women's legal rights. It was by no means a perfect movement, but it made an impact. The second wave of the women's movement peaked in the 1960s and 1970s. During this second wave, women were speaking out and writing about all areas of women's lives, such as fair pay, legal issues, family, work, violence, romance, and sexuality.

THE POWER OF WOMEN'S WORDS IN THE LAST 70 YEARS

I encourage you to dive into the writing of women who have shifted the collective conversation throughout history (there are hundreds if not thousands) but I want to highlight just a few from the last seventy years to illustrate the power a woman's words can produce.

In 1949, French author Simone de Beauvoir published *The Second Sex* in two volumes of writing that covered how women had been treated throughout history. The book made the Vatican's list of prohibited books, has been translated into forty languages, and is credited with helping to spark the second wave of the women's movement.

In 1963, Betty Friedan published *The Feminine Mystique*. Friedan wrote about how women (at that moment in time) were unsatisfied with their lives as housewives. She argued, after much research, that women could no longer ignore a voice within them that was telling them that they wanted something more out of their lives. Though the book doesn't speak for all women (it focused on middle-class white women), *The Feminine Mystique* became the bestselling nonfiction book of 1964 with over one million copies sold, and it is considered to be one of the most influential books of the twentieth century.

In 1969, Maya Angelou published her now-famous autobiography, *I Know Why the Caged Bird Sings*. Though this is more memoir/narrative storytelling, I include this book because its impact continues to be felt today. This beautifully written coming-of-age piece tackles tough subjects such as racism, trauma, and early motherhood. Angelou captures an exquisite character arc when she, with her three-year-old brother, is sent to Arkansas to live with her grandmother, faces racism and extraordinary self-doubt, and transforms herself into a self-possessed woman capable of standing up and speaking out with dignity. In 1970, it was nominated for a National Book Award; it has been published in many languages and has never been out of print.

In 1973, the Boston Women's Health Book Collective published, *Our Bodies, Ourselves.* Dynamic and groundbreaking, this book helped to change the conversation for women and their health care. Once discouraged from asking questions about their own health, the women of the Boston Women's Health Book Collective sought to change the conversation. Women shared (for one of the first times in print) deeply honest personal narratives to inform and empower one another. Over four million copies have been sold since its original publication. *Our Bodies, Ourselves* encouraged women to ask questions, tell their stories, and claim the medical care they deserved.

In 1984, Audre Lorde published *Sister Outsider*. This brave and compelling book discusses the complex intersectional identity of being a black female lesbian, as well as tough topics like ageism, war, love, police brutality, and violence against women. Her words sparked important conversations that continue to this day. Lorde became New York's Poet Laureate in 1991 and many consider *Sister Outsider* to be required reading in cultural theory and women's studies programs across the country.

Side note: I was so inspired by all of my research on female thinkers (from all walks of life, all over the world, and for centuries) that I had to stop myself from writing more. In fact, I had to put aside fifty pages of work that I realized belonged in another book on female thought leaders over the centuries. In Appendix 2 of this book (page 320), however, I do offer you a list of a few of the amazing women mentioned here and the books I recommend by or about them.

But We Do Write, We Do Speak Out. So Why Are We Still Underselling Ourselves?

One day, not so long ago in a writing class, a brilliant forty-six-year-old woman said to me, "I've sort of been waiting for the right moment to write my book."

"How long have you been waiting?" I asked.

"Hmm," she said as she thought. "For about seventeen years."

I hear this sentiment all the time. Women are waiting for *just the right time* to launch their writing career or get all their brilliance down on paper. I was about to open up the discussion for ideas when a feisty twenty-year-old woman shouted out,

"What is wrong with us? I don't get what's taking so long! Why are we still, after all of these years, underselling ourselves?"

It's easy for me to answer that question. In fact, I am repeating myself. But that's because it's an important concept.

Trust. Trust. Trust.

Trust that you are worthy. Trust that you have something valid to say. Trust that the world is ready for your words, your leadership. Trust that we are here to applaud you. Trust that the time is, indeed, right now.

Where We Can Go Together

An Exciting Trend

> *Even though prospects are dismal for women in traditional leadership roles, there's an interesting new leadership industry where women are dominating— thought leadership. Thanks to the internet and the marketing tools it provides to entrepreneurs and bloggers; we're seeing the rise of the guru.*

—Erin McKelle, *Huffington Post*

From my vantage point, women who claim their thought leader status are part of a slow-but-mighty movement. Book by book, author by author, women are beginning to find their voices, maybe even their leadership mojo, through writing. And the marketplace is responding positively. My research inspired me to investigate the popularity of female thought leaders who were boldly and unapologetically sharing their expertise.

I dove into the works of thought leaders like Brené Brown, Anne Lamott, Sheryl Sandberg, Maya Angelou, Arianna Huffington, Julia Cameron, Iyanla Vanzant, Byron Katie, Gloria Steinem, Marianne Williamson, Shonda Rhimes, Tara Mohr, Elizabeth Gilbert, Martha Beck, Glennon Doyle, Caroline Myss, Mika Brzezinski, Amy Cuddy, Louise Hay, and Susan Cain (and, oh, so many more), who were all speaking to the masses.

Look at just a few of the bestselling titles written by women in today's marketplace:

> *Knowing Your Value: Women, Money, and Getting What You're Worth* by Mika Brzezinski
>
> *#GIRLBOSS* by Sophia Amoruso
>
> *Lean In: Women, Work, and the Will to Lead* by Sheryl Sandberg

Rage Becomes Her: The Power of Women's Anger by Soraya Chemaly

Daring Greatly: How the Courage to Be Vulnerable Transforms the Way We Live, Love, Parent, and Lead by Brené Brown

Girl Positive: How Girls Are Shaping a New World by Tatiana Fraser and Caia Hagel

Dear Ijeawele, or a Feminist Manifesto in Fifteen Suggestions by Chimamanda Ngozi Adichie

Playing Big: Practical Wisdom for Women Who Want to Speak Up, Create, and Lead by Tara Mohr

You Are a Badass: How to Stop Doubting Your Greatness and Start Living an Awesome Life by Jen Sincero

A Good Time to Be a Girl: Don't Lean In, Change the System by Helena Morrissey

What do all these titles tell you? Women are seeking permission to believe in their greatness.

Here is my thinking. Instead of waiting for a sign, signal, or a well-lit path, let's take a page out of Elizabeth Cady Stanton's book and declare that the person is you and the time is now.

Are You As Impatient As I Am?

In researching this book, I interviewed a lot of women. I especially loved interviewing women who run national networking sites. My favorite interview was with Kristy Wallace of Ellevate Network in New York. I asked what trends she was seeing for women. Here is how the conversation went.

"What do you mean?" she asked.

"I mean, do you think women will start to see significant changes or real traction in the next twenty years, thirty years, more?"

She paused. Then in her no-nonsense New York-accent, she said, "I'm not usually optimistic, but I'm going to go with two years."

"Two years?" I squealed. "What?"

"Yep, two years." She went on to explain that there has been a wave of women taking ownership of their lives and careers for a while now. She said that women are catching fire. She added, "There is motivation like I have never seen. And the world will start to see the impact of that very, very soon." (Ellevate is pretty cool by the way; I love the podcast.)

I hung up the phone and did a little dance. She confirmed what I was feeling. We are currently in a women's wave—a wave of facing down shame, owning our vulnerability and power, finding our voices, and experiencing the joy of running the world. (Or at least our corner of the world.)

If you are reading this paragraph and are sitting on the fence, hop down and join us. Why? Because I have had the experience over and over, where once a woman started down the path of believing in her voice, she not only was able to change her own life but the lives of many around her.

Know that it is normal to be afraid, to have a darker part of us that leads to not-so-great places. Places where we can stew in fear, doubt, anger, resentment, and hatred—you name it. When it comes to writing, it often shows up as the part of us that tells us we can't do it. That we are not strong enough, worthy enough, or talented enough; you get the picture. The trick to moving forward is that you feel the fear, maybe even stare it in the face, but do it anyway. The trick is not to stuff it down or pretend that the darker side doesn't exist.

I want this to be clear. You don't need to change a thing about yourself or shove yourself over to some imaginary place of total confidence. You are allowed to feel good and bad, excited and terrified. I call this "holding hands with the shadow." You don't have to deny the part of yourself that may have real and valid things to say, and you aren't putting yourself down for being afraid (all humans are afraid). By holding hands with the shadow, you can acknowledge that fear may exist, and it may even have things to say from time to time, but it can't stop you from moving toward your dreams.

It can be scary to think of owning your power or wondering how your ideas will be met in the marketplace. I get it. But in my experience, there is a far greater cost to never knowing what could be, to never having trusted your brilliance or shared that spark in your soul.

Get Comfortable Starting a Revolution

So, I was in this mastermind group for about ten minutes. I wasn't the best mastermind participant. I feel I made three big offenses. One, the group wanted me to narrow down my goals to one; I couldn't. I had four goals. Four glorious goals that I loved. Two, there was a "mansplainer" in the group, and I casually mentioned that I thought he should read Rebecca Solnit's book, *Men Explain Things to Me*, to help cure him. My third offense was that I said I wanted to start a revolution to help women to feel more empowered by using their words. Someone in the group responded with a funny (or snarky) comment that looked like this:

Marni's To-Do List for Thursday

1. Buy eggs
2. Change cat litter
3. Begin revolution
4. Pay phone bill

At first, I laughed. Then, I slowly realized that I liked that to-do list. Every day since, I have put "continue revolution" on my daily to-do list.

Q: Hey, Marni, What Is a Mastermind Group?

A: Mastermind groups are being held all around the world in various formats. The goal is to create a peer-to-peer support group where you can help one another to reach new goals, break through creative blocks, or up your professional game. Groups can be conducted online or in person. Sometimes peer-to-peer only and sometimes professionally led, each mastermind group (or group leader) creates their own rules. The term was coined in 1925 in the book, *The Law of Success* by Napoleon Hill. He expanded on the idea in his 1937 book, *Think and Grow Rich*.

YOU, the Essential Component

I've finally stopped running away from myself.
Who else is there better to be?

—Goldie Hawn

What makes all of your ideas fresh and unique? They travel through YOU. How you see the world and then interpret what you see sets you apart. And guess what? We, readers, crave your unique point of view. Sometimes when I start working with a thought leader, their initial instinct is to write in a sterile, clinical, or journalistic tone. But the truth is that we want personality. We delight in creative interpretations. So, don't leave your personality out of this. Use your experiences, your humor, your honesty, your spirit. Share them all with us, and we will be drawn to your ideas even more.

Creating a Sacred Writing Space

If you struggle with the fear of jumping in, I highly suggest you take a few moments and create a sacred writing space just for yourself. Allow "sacred writing space" to mean whatever it means to you. My sacred writing space is a cluttered mess with some beautiful candles and a few treasured gifts from students. A client of mine took over a large walk-in closet and made it a palace of books and inspirational quotes. A writer friend of mine created a space in her bedroom that overlooks her garden. She tries to put fresh flowers on her desk as often as she can. No matter what kind of space you create, the important action here is that you are officially creating a space in your life dedicated to the practice of writing. Think of it as a space where you get to dream without limits. How might you decorate a space like that?

What About Male Thought Leaders?

You are welcome too! The tools in this book are for everyone. I just happen to have a personal passion for empowering female thought leaders. But do not take this in any way as a slight or judgment against men. Men are awesome. (I am married to a good one and I am trying to raise a good one.) The concepts I share in this book are all equal opportunity offerings.

Okay, I'm Ready to Do This, but HOW EXACTLY?

My goal is to walk you step-by-step through the writing process. Here's a brief overview:

In Chapter 2, I will help you to create a tenacious writing routine *that works for you.*

In Chapter 3, I will teach you the nuts and bolts of nonfiction writing, including providing you with a lexicon of frequently used words, so you can better acquaint yourself with the language you will soon be speaking. I will introduce you to the three parts of a nonfiction book: front matter, body matter, and end matter.

In Chapter 4, to help you tackle the blank page, I am going to take you through two brainstorming sessions. Session One: *The Junk Drawer Dump* and Session Two: *What Do We Have Here?* During Session Two, you will begin to identify major patterns, categories, or themes. You may start to see the core thoughts of your philosophy take shape. Your chapters may even begin to take shape.

In Chapter 5, we will begin to organize your ideas by introducing you to the Three-Key Method, which includes the Promise, Premise, and Approach.

This is a Snapshot of the Three-Key Method:

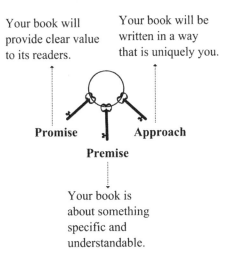

Your book will provide clear value to its readers.

Your book will be written in a way that is uniquely you.

Promise

Approach

Premise

Your book is about something specific and understandable.

The Three Keys will help you to examine *WHAT* you are writing about, *WHY* you are writing about it, and *HOW* you will write about it.

In Chapter 6, we will dive in a little deeper into Key #1 and discuss the promise of your book. This is essentially the *why* of your book. Think of it this way: *Why should a reader pick up your book?*

In Chapter 7, we will dive in a little deeper into Key #2 and discuss the premise, or the *what* of your book. This is where we find a way to define the core ideas of your book by asking, *what exactly is this book about anyway?*

In Chapter 8, we will dive a little deeper into Key #3 and discuss your approach as a writer. We will address how the information will be presented to the reader. In this chapter, as you start to think of how you will be making the book your own, I will introduce three popular Thought Leader Templates. You will answer the question, *who is the star of my show?*

In Chapter 9, I will provide you with my "17 Tips to Avoid the Snake Holes and Boulders," otherwise known as my top nonfiction writing tips for female thought leaders.

In Chapter 10, you will be introduced to an overview of the Dynamic Thought Leader Templates as well as an overview of how to craft your chapters.

In Chapter 11, you will learn all about the Big Ideas Template.

In Chapter 12, you will learn all about the Stories Template.

In Chapter 13, you will learn all about the Plan-of-Action Template.

In Chapter 14, I will ask you to release your need to learn all the rules and do it all "right," and connect with the initial spark that made you want to write your book. I will encourage you to use your honest, real, and unique personal writing voice so that your reader will come to know you and want to read everything you write.

In Chapter 15, we will discuss what makes an effective title, and I will teach you how to put your title through the title test.

In Chapter 16, I will show you how to keep yourself on track during the words-on-the-page stage. Utilizing a writing calendar and a commitment to your tenacious writing routine, you will brainstorm

- a target date for your first draft,
- an accountability program that includes Sunday-night-check-ins, and
- reward stations.

I want to encourage you to take your time and enjoy each step of the process.

In Chapter 17, we will cover some of the most frequently asked questions I receive as a writing coach. I will offer ideas to tackle those issues and to keep you moving.

In the last chapter, Chapter 18, I will have a difficult time ending the book. (I always hate goodbyes.)

But wait, there's more!

I'm excited to share a bonus chapter, *What's Branding Got to Do With It,* by Master Brander Jeniffer Thompson. In this chapter, Jeniffer will offer you ten concrete steps you can take today toward using your book as an integral part of your brand.

Know that I am right next to you through all of this. After all, it's much more fun to roar together.

Yes, You.
Yes, Now.

Permission Slip to

ROAR

I hereby give myself permission to roar. I will allow myself to listen to my still, small voice of intuition, to own my thoughts, and to get them all down on paper. I will work each day to bring my book to life using my humor, courage, and passion. I will be okay with making mistakes and fumbling through this process. I accept the idea that to be on fire, I have to kick my own ass sometimes. I embrace my talents and will allow my brilliance to shine. I say yes to me. I say yes to right now.

_____   _____

Signature   Date

Bite-Sized Thoughts for Chapter 1

1. Yes, you are a thought leader, my friend. We need your voice, and we need your voice now. Our culture is hungry for authentic female voices sharing their wisdom and speaking their truth.

2. Currently, in almost every industry in the United States, women are underrepresented.

3. Currently, there is also an exciting trend. Book by book, author by author, women are beginning to find their voices, maybe even their leadership mojo, through writing.

4. This book will take you through the Three-Key Method that will help you to examine the Promise—*WHAT* you are writing about, the Premise—*WHY* you are writing about it, and the Approach—*HOW* you will write about it.

5. If you are still working on finding the nerve (or the trust) to write your book, then start by creating a sacred space in your heart for your book. Spend time daily nurturing that creative space. Then sign the permission slip to roar and jump in with a warrior's heart.

CHAPTER 2

CREATING A TENACIOUS WRITING ROUTINE

Watching Bonobos Build Their Nests

So, it's an exciting Saturday night at our house, and I'm watching the Nature Channel with my son. I'm trying to engage him because I know if I don't, he will want to watch the zombie movie on another channel. (Zombie movies = nightmares in our home, so, we try to steer clear.) Anyway, I start paying attention to these bonobos in the Congo who are gathering and bending tree branches at sunset. It looked as if they were building nests. Then it became clear; they were indeed, totally building nests.

"I can't believe that monkeys build nests," I say. "How could I live this long on the planet and not know that?"

"Duh, Mom, they build nests for all sorts of things. Sleeping, eating, and even if they want to get away from the other guys."

My son was right. We both leaned in as the narrator shared that bonobos build nests for resting, gathering, feeding, grooming, sleeping, all sorts of things. At this particular moment, the sun was setting, and it was time for the bonobos to build their nightly nest. One bonobo was hastily building his nest near the trunk of the tree. Another was slowly folding down certain branches, carefully constructing her nest at the top of an upright tree. Another was cleverly using the tops of two trees as a base. And yet another few huddled near the middle of the largest tree to work together as they selected branches they might use.

The next day, I was teaching a large writing class, and we walked outside to write in the sunshine. I gave the writers a prompt and then told them they had twenty minutes to write. Off they went. One person moved swiftly to the trunk of a small tree and positioned all his writing gear around him in a circle. Another writer spread out under a large umbrella, moving the cushions around for maximum comfort. A third student walked to the edge of a patio and slowly pulled out noise-canceling headphones and opened her laptop to write in independent quiet. A final few gathered near the base of the largest tree and worked together to lay down blankets before they sat.

Damn. We're all bonobos.

So, the time has come to set up your writing nest.

If you have never written before, this may feel foreign to you. But it's important to take a moment to assess what works for you, as it will help you to create something sustainable (meaning for more than a couple of weeks).

Note: In Chapter 16, we will pull it all together. You will be introduced to several different ways of creating a writing calendar. A tenacious writing routine and a clear writing calendar is a winning combination.

Enjoy the Messy Process

Writing a Book Is Messy

I know, you want there to be a simple formula. I can help you a bit there. I have broken down the information in this book in ways that I think will make it easy and fun. I have provided you with three nonfiction templates in Chapters 11 through 13. But there is no way around it; writing a book is often just get-your-hands-in-the-dirt messy. That is, if you are doing it right.

Why do I tell you all of this? I want you to know that you are absolutely, and wonderfully, normal if (and when) the process confuses you from time to time.

Remember how fun it was to get messy?

We forget this as adults, but remember what it was like to get all covered in dirt when you were little? Or jump in the rain puddles? Or make all the water splash outside the tub? Or make mud pies or messy sandcastles? All that was fun because you were in the moment, building, or making something, or bucking what you should have been doing.

Writing a book can be a lot like that.

Writing a book can be play.

So, put on your galoshes, or, heck, no shoes at all, and come jump in a book-writing puddle with me.

Creating a Tenacious Writing Routine That Works for You

As we work to set you up for writing success, it's important to clarify—well, declare (I kinda like that word as you know)—your intentions with a clear writing routine. First, let's take a look at how you might work best.

What Kind of Writer Are You? Planner or Pantser?

In some ways, we, writers are alike (the self-doubt, the short attention span, the procrastination), and in some ways, we are unique. Some writers like to outline their books from top to bottom before getting to the words-on-the-page stage. Some writers want to sit down and pour words out to their hearts' content.

Planners → Outline their material before writing

Pantsers → Fly by the seat of their pants

See If You Can Identify What Kind of Writer You Are

1. The Engineer   →   All Plan, No Pants
2. The Architect   →   Mostly Plan, Smidge of Pants
3. The Buddha   →   Half Plan, Half Pants
4. The Intuitive   →   Mostly Pants, Smidge of Plan
5. The Free Spirit →   All Pants, No Plan

If you are a 3 → You are most likely balancing the right amount of concrete planning with free-flowing pouring.

If you are a 1 or a 2 → Be open to new ideas coming through during the words-on-the-page stage. Writing is a fluid art. Your best-laid plan may not work, and, ironically, a better idea might pop up. Be available to listen to the soul of the work.

If you are a 4 or a 5 → Try not to get attached to everything you write. See your first draft as part of the brainstorming stage. Be available to the lesson that your first idea may not be your ultimate and best idea. (Date, but do not marry your ideas yet.)

Uncover Your Creative Process

How do you work? How do you come up with ideas? How and when are you the most consistent? What promotes inspiration within you? What makes you want to write?

To be tenacious, you need to know the way your creative process works.

If you don't know your particular creative process, try watching yourself. Observe how you do housework, garden, eat, raise a family, fix something, paint, organize work, and interact with clients. Are you highly organized? Do you do one thing at a time?

Do you put blinders on and focus like mad? Do you accomplish things in small pieces? Do you get lost in your work for hours at a time? Do you have any rituals? What are your habits, your patterns?

No matter what your process is, you do have one. Bottom line: Learn to perform your creative routine without question, over and over, and, you will produce results. (This is tenacity.)

Focus Is a Thought Leader's Superpower

It's no secret that we live in a society filled with endless distractions. If we get bored, we move on to the next shiny attraction. I have met with many a writer who has three half-completed books. All stuck in files on her computer. She gets excited about an idea, jumps in, then, in the middle, she gets a little bored, fidgety, or doubtful. So, she sets that project aside for the next idea, which seems ever-so-alluring.

During this process, you will undoubtedly get bored, fidgety, or doubtful. Learn to take a deep breath, and then stay the course.

I also find that women struggle to give themselves permission to put their writing first (or, at least, close to the top of the list). If you resemble this remark, it may take practice to keep putting your writing needs at the top of that list.

To-Do List

1. MY WRITING
2. Dishes
3. Client call
4. Edit client's book
5. Take Ben to soccer
6. Continue revolution
7. Take the car in to find out what is leaking all over the driveway

Writing Through Chaos

A few weeks back, on a Sunday morning, I told my husband and son that it was going to be my quiet writing morning. I told them that I would see them in the afternoon, but that I would be writing for two hours solid—at least. While both are loving, talented, funny, and brilliant people, they don't like it when I sequester myself away.

So, as I opened my laptop to begin work, my son came in to show me a YouTube video that I just had to see right then and there. Behind him was my husband, asking what we would be doing for dinner (it was 9:00 a.m.). Then the phone rang, and rang, and rang. Next, two text messages pinged. At that moment our extremely wonderful and loud cat, Mr. Beef, entered my office and puked up some string. I politely looked at all of them, each waiting for my attention.

As I was cleaning up the cat's gift, I walked into the kitchen. I was stunned by the mess, and thought, *wow, where did all those dishes come from?* I felt pulled to start cleaning but resisted, knowing that the kitchen mess would be there when I was finished with my writing session. As I moved back to my office, my husband wanted to chat about a movie he was working on, and my son had a new balancing trick he felt I needed to see. But, I politely told my husband and son that I would be available in two hours, turned off my phone, and shut the door.

It was not easy. But I had promised myself focused writing time. For me, focused writing time comes in spurts. When I get it, I jump on it.

When you do persist, commit, and find focus, there is so much waiting for you. The person who pushes through the anxiety, fear, and distractions to focus on completing just one project at a time can soar.

I want to be clear here. There will be times that you will have to demand the time it will take to complete your book. People may not understand upfront, but trust me, when they are at your book launch party, and you are signing a book for them, they will get it.

If you find you suffer from distracted thinking:

Study yourself.

What pulls you off your track?

Get clear with yourself. Is it work, hobbies, lack of time, social media, lack of a routine, anxiety, loneliness, poor diet, lack of sleep, family demands, health, or obligations?

Then, try the Remove-and-Add approach.

Remove: What obstacles are in your way? How many of them can you REMOVE? If you have too many demands on your time, seek out help or learn to say no. Take yourself off committees or boards. If you have too many hobbies that take your attention, decide that you will take six months to complete your vision and then return to your hobbies.

Add: Now take a moment to assess what you can ADD to your life that will help you jump over those hurdles. If you write half a book and it stays hidden in a file on your computer, find yourself a class, a regular writing group, or a writing coach that can hold you accountable. If you find you get lonely, seek out a writing community online or in person, read books like *The Gifts of Imperfection* by Brené Brown (Brown has an excellent anxiety-detox routine), *The Power of Habit* by Charles Duhigg, or *Grit* by Angela Duckworth. Bottom line: Add any elements that will increase your accountability.

Focus pays off. Demand it.

Planning and Pouring

You will be doing two kinds of writing sessions as you work on your book: planning and pouring.

Planning involves diving into a conscious-thinking state, one where you will be looking over the templates, figuring out what your chapter recipes will be, unearthing how you will begin and end, and deciding how you want to structure your book.

Pouring involves turning on the tap and allowing all of your ideas to flow out freely. Pouring involves *not thinking* so much, or not thinking at all. In fact, you would not believe how often I tell a client to "stop thinking so much."

Here's how a pouring session works. You sit down at the computer, or with a notebook, and you just write down your stream of consciousness. Get it all out. Yep, every odd, and wacky, and incomplete thought in your head. Truth be told, you can write your entire book by pouring first, then looking over all the material, and then organizing it. If you are brand new to writing, I suggest alternating between planning sessions and pouring sessions. Allow whole sessions for your mind to run free with no limits. Then, look at what you have poured out, and see where the material might fit in your book. I see alternating between planning sessions and pouring sessions as a fun dance.

How a First Draft Gets Written

You might be wondering about the nitty-gritty aspects of writing a book and want a quick overview. Here it is. Think through your Three Keys: the Promise, the Premise, and the Approach. Then take some time. Percolate, plan, pour, daydream, and stare out the window.

(Yes, staring out the window counts.)

The Eight Stages of Writing

Many people ask me what the stages of writing to publishing look like. Meaning, how does it all work, exactly? As I've discussed, there is no one way to write a book, and writing a book is messy. Still, there is a general flow that tends to happen. Writers often move from one stage to the next in the following order. (But try not to get too caught up in doing it "right," as right is whatever process works for you.)

1. Prewriting and Planning – dreaming, doing, researching, brainstorming, pouring, choosing your template, and outlining (some writers like to work with a developmental or structural editor during this stage to help them plan)
2. Writing – words-on-the-page stage
3. Rewriting – moving the words around, filling in the holes, eliminating repetition, enhancing clarity
4. Polishing – fixing the tone, sound, and flow of words

5. Beta Readers – giving your draft to people in your target audience (not your mom or best friend) who read your draft and give notes
6. Rewriting and Polishing – reworking based on beta readers' notes
7. Editors, Editors, Editors – giving your work to an editor to line edit and copy edit (for definitions of what editors do, see page 284)
8. Publishing –
    *   Traditional: query → agent → publisher → out into the world. This can be a long process; it's not uncommon for it to take two to three years (but it's highly rewarding).
    *   Indie or hybrid: find yourself a qualified book professional to guide you or go to a hybrid publisher → your work finds its way out into the world. This can be a much quicker process (from months to less than a year).

Q: Hey, Marni! What the Heck Is a Hybrid Publisher?

A: You probably know that the publishing industry is changing almost faster than we can track. So, the definition will continue to evolve and grow. As of this writing, a hybrid publisher is one with whom you share the cost of publication, and they assist you with creating a polished product and, most importantly, they assist you with distribution. Before you sign on with a hybrid publisher, do your research to make sure they are reputable.

Some writers go through two rounds of beta readers, meaning you have two to three beta readers read a draft and then offer you notes so you can rewrite or polish. Then you have a second round of different beta readers look over the next draft and offer notes so that you can polish once more.

Some writers utilize editors or writing coaches throughout the entire process. This can greatly increase the professional quality of your book and cut down on the amount of time it takes during the rewriting stage.

I lay out these stages as a way of showing new writers the adage that writing is rewriting. Give yourself lots of leeway to get your words down on paper. You will have many opportunities to revise until you are satisfied with the finished draft.

Do I Have to Write It All in Order?

Nope. Once you have your outline, you can either "sequence it" or "Frankenstein it."

Sequencing: Writing your book in a linear fashion, taking one step at a time in sequence (first you write chapter one, then you write chapter two, then chapter three, and four and five, etc.).

Frankensteining: Writing your book one piece at a time, according to what you feel like writing that day. At the end of this process, your draft may look clunky or awkwardly stuck together, but don't worry, you will have plenty of time to smooth it out, polish it up, and make it look pretty.

At some point in the process, you will start connecting to the soul of the book. The book may even start talking to you, so pay attention and listen. This is when the writing is the most alive.

Two Reminders

Reminder 1: The fastest way to get the first draft down is to permit yourself to write a crappy first draft.

Reminder 2: **Writing is rewriting.** You will have many drafts to polish and perfect your vision. There is no perfect first draft. You will be rewriting, so let go of having to do it right the first time.

Enjoy the Journey. Allow Your Book the Time It Needs

In our snap-your-fingers-and-make-it-happen-now society, you will likely want to be done with your book yesterday. You may feel that you must write your book super-fast and complete it swiftly and easily. Wanna know who pisses me off? The people who write those "Write Your Book in 7 Days" books. Why? I am the unfortunate recipient of many of those books written in a week. And it ain't pretty. That's not to say that if you have been thinking about the book forever that you won't be able to spit it out swiftly. But here is my best advice.

Do your best to get your mind off the clock. You are going to learn a tremendous amount as you write. You will be upping your game as you research, write, and polish. So, the very process is valuable in and of itself. Furthermore, don't buy into any inner dialogue or external pressure that you are late or slow. Good books take time.

The Last Time I Wanted to Punch an Author

About a year ago, I found myself at a pretentious book signing. The author read from his book, and then he noted that he would be offering a brand new, "Write Your Book In 30 Days" workshop. The author went on to talk about the power of writing fast. Now, I had students in the crowd who had been writing their books for more than a year. Their faces scrunched in pain. I could almost hear their thoughts: *damn, why can't I write that fast? What is wrong with me?* Then, and I kid you not (I have witnesses), the author went on to tell the story of how his book was written. He explained that it was a three-and-a-half-year process. With no sense of irony. A three-and-a-half-year process. So that is more like 912 days, which is 882 days longer than the promised thirty.

Now, see here, I am in the business of teaching writing, and I genuinely love making people happy. So, I understand the pull to tell people what they want to hear. And what do people want to hear? They want to hear that they can write a high-quality piece of work in thirty days. Or sixty. Or ninety.

I know what you are thinking. *Oh no, how long will it really take me?*

Here is the honest answer. It depends.

What shortens the process? Experience, the amount of time you can devote to the book, and the length of the book. I have seen highly experienced writers turn out a short e-book in about three months. But for most, a year is a reasonable amount of time if you are dedicated.

I want to challenge the get-it-done-fast thinking in two ways.

1. Instead of getting it done fast, move toward getting it done so that your work is high quality. (Quality takes time and multiple drafts.)
2. Instead of, *where am I in the process?* move toward, *am I enjoying the process?*

I realize I am flying in the face of our culture, which is often focused on swift gratification and racking up achievements. For the sake of both quality and sanity, I invite you to enjoy every single part of the process of being a writer. The fast parts, the slow parts, the maddening parts, the exciting parts, the being-in-the-moment parts, and the see-I-did-it parts. Fall in love with all of it, and you will love your writing experience.

And guess what? You are not late. You are right on time.

In fact, you are right where you are supposed to be.

So there.

My Tenacious Writing Routine

What kind of writer I am (planner or pantser) _____

Where I work best (place) _____

When I work best (time of day) _____

How I work best (method) _____

I am going to work on taking care of myself better by _____

_____

_____

What I will REMOVE from my routine to allow more time and
space for writing_____

_____

_____

What I will ADD to my routine to encourage consistent writing
and completion of my book _____

_____

_____

I will incorporate more play into my tenacious writing routine by

_____

_____

_____

My reward system or accountability routine looks like _____

_____

_____

_____

I see myself as tenacious because _____

_____

_____

_____

Note: For the strongest writing experience, you will want to pair your tenacious writing routine with a clear writing calendar, discussed in Chapter 16.

Bite-Sized Thoughts for Chapter 2

1. DECLARE your intentions to complete your book by crafting a tenacious writing routine. Take some time to figure out how you work creatively. Find out where, when, and how you write best.

2. There are Eight Stages of Writing. Learn the stages so you will better understand
   - the path you will most likely take to write your book, and that
   - writing is rewriting.

3. Writing a book is often get-your-hands-in-the-dirt messy. Remember how fun it was to get messy?

4. A first draft can be written in a linear fashion, filling in one chapter after the next, or you can Frankenstein it (you jump around and write whatever section calls to you).

5. Don't worry about how long it takes you. To get your book done to the best of your ability, you will travel through many iterations. You are a writer. Enjoy every aspect of the process. Writing a book can be play. So play, damn it.

I am a writer.

CHAPTER 3

JUST THE FACTS, MA'AM

Taking Apart the Noodle Machine

Right after I graduated from film school, I had about three hundred jobs. Transcribing was one of them. I transcribed notes for an eclectic and successful writer, let's call him Sam, who also made noodles. Well, he *wanted* to be a professional noodle maker. He was a well-respected writer, but at that moment, he aspired to be a noodle maker. He also hated to type ("longhand all the way," he would say) so he hired me to transcribe his notes for his upcoming memoir. One day, I came into the kitchen and found him sitting amongst a variety of parts of one of his elaborate noodle makers. Odd-shaped metal pieces were strewn over the counter, the floor, and the windowsill.

"What happened?" I asked.

In a nonchalant manner, he said, "Look, Marni, if you want to make noodles for a living, then you may want to know how the noodle machine works."

I knew better than to probe further, and I nodded. Somehow it made sense. He indicated that he needed help, so for the rest of the afternoon, we sat together and figured out how to install the fettuccini attachment so that it wouldn't fall off. (Not easy.)

About three weeks later, I was transcribing his memoir. I was typing in one room while he sat in the next room writing longhand. I would comment from time to time, ask questions, make observations on the dialogue, or laugh. He told me he loved to hear my reactions. Sometimes we would talk about my reactions for hours. Analyze them. I was getting toward the middle of his story and was noticing how he was continuously ratcheting up the tension to hold the reader's interest.

"I love how you are sustaining the tension here, in this schoolyard scene right in the middle."

"Oh, you noticed that."

"Yes. But I don't understand why you are still keeping the main secret of the book from the reader. When are you going to share it?" And we launched into a discussion of tension-filled story revelations for added suspense.

Two weeks later, I had my work times mixed up, and I mistakenly arrived an hour early at his home to transcribe. I entered the house, and there was Sam. Not in the sitting room, but in the office. Happily typing away.

But he hated to type. What happened to, "Longhand all the way"? Yet there he was, tip-tapping away, transcribing much faster than I ever could. And he looked happy. Then he saw me, and he looked caught.

"Wait a second," I said. "You like typing. Now I remember, you told me so about three years ago."

"Yeah, I don't mind it." He shrugged it off. Kept typing.

I sat down. "So why are you having me do it?" I asked.

"Well, I do prefer longhand. And you're fun to have around. And you're young and naturally gifted, but also very stupid, and you want to make noodles for a living, so I figured you should intimately learn the parts of the noodle machine."

I went and kissed the top of his head. He was teaching me how to write.

Nonfiction Book Parts

We're just going to peek inside the machine for a minute. Follow me for a bit.

A Nonfiction Book Is Made Up of Three Parts

1. Front Matter
2. Body Matter (sometimes referred to as the "text")
3. End Matter (sometimes referred to as "back matter")

The front matter is usually everything before the main section (the meat) of your book. It contains the technical details of your book such as the title page, the dedication, table of contents, foreword, and introduction.

When we refer to the body matter, we are talking about the core content of your book, such as the parts, sections, and chapters.

The end matter is the optional materials at the back of the book such as the afterword, glossary, acknowledgments, appendix, and index.

The following is a mini-lexicon to better understand the different sections of your book.

Marni's Mini-Lexicon for Writing a Book: Learn Your New Language

(Don't get scared, there's a handy cheat sheet at the end of the chapter.)

Front Matter

The front matter is the first part of your book. It will contain the technical details. Often, the front matter pages are numbered in lowercase roman numerals. You will not find any page numbers on the title or the copyright pages, or blank pages (your designer or publisher will take care of all this, by the way).

The front matter is the content that appears before the main text. It consists of the book's title, the author's name, and the copyright information, and it may also include a preface or a foreword. The front matter reveals the book's structure, explains how to navigate through the material, and sets the tone.

Half-Title Page: This is the first page of your book upon which you will have your title (and only your title). No byline or subtitle here. (No need to create this page; the designer will do this.)

Series Title Page: Usually the second page of your book. You can list any of your previously published books (listed chronologically) by title on this page. Commonly, you see this page with the heading "Also by (your name)." This can appear in the front matter or the back matter.

Title Page: This page shows your full book title and the subtitle. It also includes all the authors' (and translators') names, and the name and location of the publisher.

Copyright Page: This page contains the copyright notice that includes the name of the copyright owner and the year of publication. The author is usually the copyright owner, yet it could be a group, a corporation, or an organization. This page may also include permissions, acknowledgments, and the book's publishing history as well as disclaimers. It may also include the ISBN (International Standard Book Number) and a Library of Congress number.

Copyright Attributions: This is an acknowledgment giving credit to the holder of the copyright of a certain work, often shown as "©" (for "copyright") with the year and the person's name. Attribution makes it clear that others do not own the work and appropriately gives credit where credit is due. The copyright attributions and any "reprinted by permission" disclaimers can go on the copyright page, or you can create a dedicated permissions page in the back matter.

Praise For: This is an optional page that has quotes praising the book from notable people who have read and appreciated the book.

Dedication: This is where the author can dedicate her work to a beloved friend or family member or significant person in their life. A dedication is personal. Professional acknowledgments go on the acknowledgments page or in the preface.

Table of Contents: Usually titled "Contents" only; used in nonfiction works that may have parts and chapters. You don't need a table of contents if your chapters are numbered only.

List of Illustrations: This is the page that lists all the illustrations within your book. Writers usually list the pieces that are key to the book (those that provide information or enhance the information in a certain way). You don't have to list lesser key illustrations, like those used for comic relief or as a visual aid. (Leave the page numbers to the formatting department.)

List of Tables: This is a page that will list any key tables that you may have used in your book.

Foreword: This is a piece of writing about the book itself and is often written by someone other than the author. Often an expert or a widely known figure in the field will write a foreword. A foreword serves to lend authority to your book. It may increase the book's potential for recognition or higher sales.

Preface: A preface can include why you wrote the book and can also contain acknowledgments. Some use the preface to establish their expertise and explain their qualifications or authority on the subject matter of the book.

Introduction: The introduction informs the reader about any information they might need before they read the book. While a preface usually covers the qualifications of the author, the introduction covers the material itself. This is a good place to discuss the overall concept of the book and your approach or research methods (if appropriate), and it can prepare your readers for how you have structured the book.

Body Matter

The Meat → The Main Text.

This is the bulk of your book; your content, separated into parts, sections, and chapters (in that order). The theory or heart of your book is explained in meaningful chapters and sections. This is where your Big Ideas, the Stories, and the Plan-of-Action are found. Body matter is paginated with Arabic numerals starting with the number "1" on the first page of the first chapter and continuing for the rest of the manuscript, including back matter.

After the main text (but before the back matter), many nonfiction books include a separate conclusion.

Conclusion: The ending section that summarizes the ideas, theories, and concepts presented in the book. Often includes a hope, wish, or call to action.

Back Matter

This is the content that appears after the main text. The back matter provides support materials and sources. It can consist of these elements:

Afterword: The afterword often discusses how the author came up with the idea for the book and the steps the author took to make it a reality. The afterward can be written by the author or by someone who can shed light on the content in some new or interesting manner.

Appendixes: This is where you would place any data that might help clarify or support the text. It is common in the appendix to place items like reports, sources, background research, tables, or a list of references.

Endnotes: This is often the preferred method (vs. footnotes) to cite specific quotations, to explain an important reference or comment, or to attribute the origin of an idea or phrase used in the body matter. Endnotes are arranged by chapter and listed numerically and consecutively in your body matter and endnotes citations.

Glossary: Alphabetically arranged, these are the important words in the text and their definitions. Authors often include a glossary if they are using terminology that may be new to their readers.

Bibliography or References: This section lists the sources for works that you used in your book. They are arranged alphabetically by the authors' last names.

Resources: The author can include a list of associations, groups, organizations, or websites that they think might be valuable for their reader. Readers often want to learn more about a certain subject matter, join organizations, or purchase products that you have written about in your book. The resource list provides them this access.

List of Contributors: This will be used if you have multiple authors, but only the volume editor's name appears on the title page. Arrange the author's last names alphabetically (but do not invert the name). You can also add the academic affiliations and a brief bio.

Acknowledgments: This includes your notes of appreciation to anyone who supported you through the writing process (usually covers those that helped with conceptual, editorial, moral, technical, financial, or motivational support.) Some authors choose to put this page (especially if it goes long) in the back-matter section, near the bibliography.

Index: This is an alphabetized, fairly detailed list of topics, names, places, or subject matter and the corresponding pages in which they are covered in the book.

Addendum: Sometimes used to explain updates or continuing thought on the subject matter, an addendum may also highlight inconsistencies or alternatives in thought.

A Reader's Guide: This section can contain any information that was not included in the text, like tips for educators, tips for parents, recommended reading, or an interview with the author. These topics can be broken up to stand on their own or placed together as a reader's guide. This section can also offer questions for a book club.

About the Author: This is the section where the reader gets to know a little bit more about you, the author. It is a place where you can share more of your personal story, experience, and authority as well as your social media platforms.

Call to Action: Some authors include a call to action at the end of the book that invites the reader to engage with you or join your community.

THE PARTS OF A BOOK CHEAT SHEET

Front Matter
- Half-title page
- Title page
- Copyright page
- Copyright attributions (for titles with reprinted or permissioned material)
- Praise for
- Dedication
- Table of contents
- List of illustrations
- Foreword (written by someone other than the author)
- Preface
- Introduction

Body Matter (the core content of the book)
- Parts/Sections/Chapters (in that order)
- Conclusion

End Matter (optional materials at the back of the book)
- Afterword
- Appendixes
- Endnotes
- Glossary
- Bibliography or references
- Resources
- Acknowledgments
- Index
- Reader's guide/teacher's guide/parent's guide
- About the author
- Call to action: Ways to join the author's community
- Other optional end matter:
  - Chapter from next book
  - Interview with the author
  - Book club questions
  - Other titles by the author
  - List of contributors
  - Addendum

Hey, Marni, What If?

Q: What If I Don't Want to Use All the Elements Described in the Front, Body, and End Matter?

A: You don't have to. Well, not necessarily. If you publish traditionally, your publisher will make the decisions. If you self-publish, depending upon the template that you choose, it is entirely your choice.

Q: So What Sections Are Mandatory and What Sections Are Optional?

A: While this is disputable, there are general rules of thumb. See below for what is generally mandatory and what is generally optional.

Mandatory (meaning pretty much every nonfiction book has this stuff)

- Title page
- Copyright page
- Dedication
- Table of contents
- Introduction
- Body matter
- Conclusion
- About the author (optional but highly recommended)
- **Optional**
  o Foreword
  o Praise for
  o Dedication
  o List of illustrations
  o Attribution
  o Series title page
  o List of tables

o Foreword
o Preface
o Index
o Glossary
o Notes
o Bibliography
o Resources
o Afterword
o Appendix
o Addendum
o List of contributors
o Chapter from your next book

Q: Is There Anything That Can Help Me to Decide What Optional Information I Should Include?

A: Look at books that inspire you and resemble the kind of book you would like to write. Then study the templates to see how you might want to shape your book. Certain optional elements will be obvious. For instance, if you have several contributors, it makes sense to have a list of contributors. Or if you have a wonderful author that is going to write you a foreword, you will want to include a foreword. If your book offers a lot of new language, a glossary of terms may be helpful to the reader. If someone inspired you, and you want to dedicate the work to him or her, then the dedication page would be applicable. Again, read, read, read, and study the books you love. Books you love are templates in and of themselves.

Q: But Can't I Follow My Own Structure? Set Up My Own Rules?

A: Yep. You can do whatever you want. But I'm here to teach you how to adhere to professional standards that are generally used within the industry.

Q: Won't Following a Formula Make the Book Boring? What About Originality?

A: There will still be tons of places where you can be completely original. Think about all those original words. Your audience has already come to expect a certain structure when reading a book. What the structure provides is clarity, and ease of use, for your reader.

Q: How Long Should My Book Be? How Many Words?

A: There is no exact right amount of words, but there are approximations or averages. See below for the current averages for nonfiction e-books and print books. The direction we are heading in is that books are getting shorter. (But pay attention to the marketplace; it is always changing.)

E-books
- Super-short e-books: 3,000 to 5,000 words
- Average-length e-books: 20,000 to 25,000 words

Print books
- Short print books: 30,000 words
- Average length of print books: 40,000 to 50,000 words
- Longer length print books: 75,00 to 80,000 words

Notes: This is the target word count. Your first draft will most likely be longer or shorter than your ideal length. Don't worry about length in the initial stages; just get it all down on paper. There will be time to edit and sculpt the book until it is lean, mean, and ready for the marketplace. Also, there are some content or research-rich thought leader books that are approximately 90,000 words.

Q: What If My First Draft Is Too Short?

A: That, too, is quite common. A good developmental editor or a talented writing group can help you to figure out where and how to expand. Allow the first draft to be whatever it is, then bring in fresh eyes you trust to help you flesh out your material.

But, Ma, Do I Have to Make a Plan?

Probably the most common question I get asked is this:

Q: Can't I Just Sit Down and Write Whatever Wants to Come out? Do I Need to Plan It out?

A: Yes, you can just pour it all out. But, if possible, I want you to think it through first (even just a bit). Thinking it through is writing! In my work, I have found that the more a person made a plan that they loved, the less they had to rewrite. Planning often saves years of rewriting. (Yeah, years.)

HOWEVER, if the only way that you will start writing is to write with no structure whatsoever, then I say go for it. If any aspect of the process stops you from writing, move in a different direction. You want to be a train on the move. So, get your thoughts out on paper. You can always assemble them in a way that feels dynamic and is structurally sound at a later date. I am a big planner. I love to map things out. But in my work with writers who experience a lot of anxiety, planning and organizing don't always work.

If you are prone to a lot of anxiety when it comes to writing, get your thoughts down on the page. Pour it all out. No censor, no rules. You do not want to think yourself into circles or out of writing in the first place. Pour out the ideas, and then use this book to organize your raw material. You can do this.

If you tend to be overconfident when it comes to writing, then realize that this is a whole other type of bird. It's wonderful to be confident, but some new writers are so confident that they don't take the time they need to make a plan. Remember, you want a book filled with your *best* ideas, not simply your *first* ideas. Overconfident writers tend to fall in love with their original words once they are on the page and they have a harder time rewriting. So, if you fit into this category (and, yes, all that delicious confidence will be helpful for your entire career), it's important to look over the templates and make an outline.

Your job right now is to focus on the body matter. It's good to know the parts of the book. But, for our purposes, you don't need to worry about the front and end matter, at least not right now. Spend your time and energy on crafting the body matter. That is the part that can only be done by you.

Bite-Sized Thoughts for Chapter 3

1. A nonfiction book is made up of three parts: front matter, body matter, and end matter.

2. The front matter is everything before the main section (the body matter) of your book. It contains the technical details of your book such as the title page, dedication, table of contents, foreword, and introduction.

3. The body matter contains the core content of your book, such as the parts, sections, and chapters.

4. The end matter contains optional materials at the back of the book, such as the afterword, the appendix, the glossary, and the index.

5. Don't worry about the front and end matter. Your job right now is to focus on the body matter, which is truly the heart and soul of your book.

CHAPTER 4

GET ROLLING WITH TWO BRAINSTORMING SESSIONS

Stuffed With Good Ideas That Won't Come out

Jenny had been my good friend since childhood. She was an accomplished, well-respected businesswoman who worked from sunup to sundown. For years, she had wanted to write a book about how workaholics can create a healthier lifestyle. About ten years earlier, Jenny was obese, unhealthy, and in trouble with her doctors. They told her to make some drastic changes or face consequences like a heart attack or a stroke. She explained that she was at work from early morning to late at night and that she didn't have time to eat healthy or exercise. Her doctor noted that the last woman that came in with her profile had a heart attack within a week.

Jenny knew she was not going to suddenly stop being a workaholic. She would tell me, "Being a workaholic is what I do, and I'm not going to stop, but if I don't get healthier, my life is in danger." It didn't happen overnight, but slowly, she began looking at her lifestyle and making small changes here and there. Soon, these small changes added up to weight loss, increased energy, and a healthier body and mind.

Now, a decade later, she was a fitness guru and health coach. She had been dreaming about writing a book about how she changed her life successfully while still remaining a workaholic. Jenny finally made an appointment with me to get started on her book. As I sat in my home office waiting for her to show up, she called in a bit of a panic. "I can't do it," she said. "I just don't think I can do it, and I don't know why." Confused as to what had caused her anxiety, I decided to make a writing coach house call. I entered her house and found Jenny standing by the window in her living room, just sort of, well, frozen.

"You okay?" I asked.

"I'm not sure," she said.

I asked her to sit down and tell me what was wrong. She told me that she cared so deeply about her material, but that she felt like all her ideas were stuck in her throat. She said, "It's like my brain is so stuffed with good ideas, I can feel and hear them, but then I go to sit down and write to get them all down, and my fingers don't move. Nothing comes out." I told Jenny not to worry, that we would take a few breaths, make some tea, and get to work brainstorming.

Introduction to Brainstorming

Jenny was not alone. I have met with many a writer who felt "stuffed with good ideas" but was unable to get them down on paper. These women tend to have tremendous experience, expertise, and wisdom. But when they arrive at the blank page, they find that a clutching sensation creeps up. Panic seeps in along with questions like these

- *Where do I start?*
- *How do I organize my ideas and make it all make sense?*
- *How do I know what information goes where?*

That panic can build up and result in what people call writers block. So, what to do?

First, let's take a big, collective deep breath together. (Really, do it!)

Next, take a step back and put on your galoshes. Remember, the ones I asked you to put aside when I told you we were going to jump into a messy puddle together? Well, the time is now. We are about to jump into a puddle of ideas and splash around. It's time to brainstorm.

I am going to walk you through two brainstorming sessions, though you can do as many as you want, and if you find a certain style of brainstorming valuable, feel free to repeat it. Think of it like organizing a junk drawer. First, we must dump all of the contents out, and then we can investigate what's in there.

- Brainstorm Session One: *The Junk Drawer Dump*
- Brainstorm Session Two: *What Do We Have Here?*

The first brainstorming session is called: *The Junk Drawer Dump*. The goal here is to dump ALL of your ideas out onto the page. Even if they seem random, bizarre, confusing, scattered, unimpressive, chaotic, or strange. So yes, all ideas count.

The second brainstorming session is called: *What Do We Have Here?* This is where you look at everything in the junk drawer and see if you can start creating categories. In a typical junk drawer, you may find rubber bands, paper clips, loose change, receipts, pens and pencils, etc. If you want to organize the drawer, you will put all the rubber bands together in one pile, all the change in another pile, and all the pens and pencils in another pile. The same goes for your ideas. Once they are all out there, take a good long look at all of your thoughts, whims, and musings. Then ask, *can I put them together in piles or categories?* Let's look at how Jenny walked through the process.

Jenny's Brainstorming Session One:
Junk Drawer Dump

For her first brainstorming session, I asked Jenny to turn off her thinking brain entirely. I handed her pen and paper and gave her the prompt "I want my book to be about ...." Jenny panicked for a few minutes, began to scribble, and then, in no time, she poured out five pages full of her raw ideas. They covered topics such as hating exercise and avoiding the gym because she could only go when it was super crowded, research about mastering her metabolism, being too sedentary during her day, grabbing fast food for almost every meal, standing up at work instead of sitting, making Sunday the day she planned her meals for the week, resources for healthy cooking when you have no time, the beauty of healthy frozen meals in a pinch, lunchtime workouts, research about taking the stairs more often and walking more in general, how to avoid stress eating, obstacles like office parties and dinners with clients, finding an office workout buddy, and the most efficient workout for busy people. Her thoughts were both interesting and all over the place. The sentences were incomplete and choppy. Her ideas were unfinished and rambling. She scribbled, mused, and repeated herself. And guess what? The brainstorming session had been a complete success because she allowed this session to be sloppy and fun. It was a success because her ideas were now out of her head and on paper.

Jenny's Brainstorming Session Two:
What Do We Have Here?

The next day, Jenny and I sat down together to look over all her pages. Within ten minutes, we noticed that her ideas fit into categories.

She Came Up With the Following Categories for Her Book

- Steps to go from sedentary to moving. What to do if you hate to leave your desk
- Steps to go from unplanned eating to planned eating
- The latest research
- The biggest obstacles busy people face
- Helpful resources for workaholics who hate to reach out for help

While Jenny liked the general direction, she wanted more organization. She gave herself a week to dream about how to organize the material. She realized that she had research for both exercise and healthy eating that she wanted to share with the reader. She also wanted to talk about common obstacles and helpful resources when discussing healthy eating and moving more. Finally, she decided that there was no one-size-fits-all plan. She had worked with many women who had to customize their new habits to make them stick.

The Next Day, While Walking Her Dog, She Realized Her Book Could Look Like This

- Section One: Steps to Go From Sedentary to Moving. What to Do If Your Desk Is Your Comfort Zone.
  - The Latest Research
  - The Biggest Obstacles
  - Helpful Resources
  - My Personalized Plan

- Section Two: Steps to Go From Unplanned Eating to Planned Eating. What to Do If McDonald's Is Your Personal Chef.
  - The Latest Research
  - The Biggest Obstacles
  - Helpful Resources
  - My Personalized Plan

Jenny knew that she wanted to craft specific steps from her brainstorming, but she wasn't yet ready to complete that task. However, she had done enough basic brainstorming to wrap her mind around her big ideas. The second brainstorming session had been a success because the pillars of her book had begun to emerge.

Now, it's your turn to brainstorm.

Two Brainstorming Sessions Worksheet

This is going to be fun. Here's what I want you to do. With no rhyme or reason, no critical thought process, and no restrictions whatsoever, I want you to pour out all of your ideas. Use the prompt, "My book is about…." And then, turn on the tap and pour it all out.

Use these worksheets to just let your mind run free.

Brainstorm Session One:
The Junk Drawer Dump

My book is about _____

_____

_____

_____

_____

_____

_____

_____

_____

_____

Tip: Take some time between brainstorming sessions. Your subconscious needs some time to work. Allow time for all the ideas, thoughts, and feelings to percolate, bounce around, dance a bit, and then settle down.

Once you have allowed some thinking time (yes, staring out the window counts), then move on to the next brainstorming session.

Brainstorm Session Two:
What Do We Have Here?

After you have taken a little break, let's take a look at all of those random thoughts and ideas that you got down on paper. What do you see or notice? Anything jump out at you?

Do you see these?

- Patterns
- Similarities
- Umbrella themes—these are larger ideas that smaller ideas can fit into. Example: "Colors" is an umbrella theme. "Red," "blue," and "yellow" are ideas that can go under that umbrella.

What may emerge?

- A system or steps in a system
- A tendency toward telling stories
- An overall call to action for your reader
- The main concepts, pillars, themes, or philosophies of your thinking
- Chapter titles
- Categories or sections
- Key thoughts of your philosophy

When I look over all of my ideas, I notice _____

_____

_____

_____

_____

_____

_____

_____

_____

_____

_____

_____

_____

Q: What Do I Do If All I See Is a Bunch of Random Ideas?

A: Don't rush it. Allow your ideas to marinate. Find your sounding boards. Talk to trusted friends, writing groups, and mentors. Toss your ideas around. Write in a journal to explore your thoughts further. A good sounding board can be priceless. Writers often become nervous about not finding their system or core concepts fast enough. Fast simply doesn't matter. What matters are that these ideas authentically reflect who you are and what you want to say.

Pay special attention to → the way you are drawn to write your book. This will help you determine which template to use, as you'll learn about in Chapters 11–13. If you tend toward creating a shift in thinking, you may want to consider the Big Ideas Template. If you are drawn toward storytelling, you will want to consider the Stories Template. If you have a clear system that you are writing about, you will want to look at the Plan-of-Action Template.

Advanced Brainstorming: The Annoying Gift That Is Writing a Book Proposal

Once you have done your initial brainstorming sessions and walked yourself through the Three Keys (which you'll learn about in the next chapter) it may help to write a book proposal. Guy Kawasaki, in his book, *APE Author, Publisher, Entrepreneur*, brings an important recipe to the forefront. He states that engaging in the process of writing a book, if you are going to self-publish (and even if you are not), is a lot like being an entrepreneur.

Writing a book proposal, even if it is for yourself, can help you to think through the book's entire presentation from beginning concept to getting your book into the hands of the readers. It can help you understand how you will function as an entrepreneur once your book has been published. Writing the book proposal and taking on the role of entrepreneur (or authorpreneur), are cures for the "I have hundreds of my unsold books in my garage and I don't know what to do with them" syndrome.

Q: Hey, Marni, What's a Book Proposal?

A: A book proposal is a valuable tool that writers use to sell their nonfiction books. The book proposal explains why your book is a salable product for the current marketplace. Think of it as a business plan. Many writers write the book proposal first along with a few sample chapters (instead of writing the whole book) to gain interest. If a publisher likes what they see in the proposal, they may pay you to write your entire book.

Q: About How Long Is a Book Proposal?

A: The length can vary. The approximate length is ten to twenty-five pages, not including sample chapters. They can run up to fifty pages when you include sample chapters.

Q: Who Does a Book Proposal Go to?

A: If you want to publish traditionally, your proposal will go to query agents. If you want to self-publish, your proposal can be one of your guides for the promotion and marketing of your book.

Q: What If I'm Not Going to Send It to an Agent—Should I Still Write One?

A: I would still recommend preparing an informal book proposal. It will help you to think through the major concepts you want to communicate and the titles that are comparable to your own, and to take into account the people that will be your targeted readers.

Here is the general outline for a successful nonfiction book proposal. I encourage you to sketch your answers.

Overview

- Target audience: Who do you think are the people who will be purchasing your book? Why will they be compelled to buy it? Avoid broad arguments; an agent or publisher wants to understand why a certain demographic will want to purchase your book. They want to visualize your reader and get a sense of how you might be able to reach them.
- Competitive title analysis: Point out similar books that are out there, and why yours is different and valuable. Think of including approximately six to ten titles, unless you have such a specialized topic that there is a targeted and smaller audience.
- Marketing plan: A more detailed discussion of how you will attempt to reach your target audience and sell your book.
- Author bio
- Chapter outline
- Sample chapters

Often, I get emails from frustrated writers who have spent years on their book, yet, somehow, they expected to press publish, and the world would take notice. The reality is that we live in a crowded, noisy publishing market. Some of these writers tell me they don't have smart phones, will never use social marketing, hate Facebook, didn't get in the business to be a promoter, and the like. I get it. It can feel like putting on an uncomfortable hat at first. Most writers, truth be told, do not want to have anything to do with the PR and marketing. It simply is not their natural skill set. And furthermore, many writers tell me that they wouldn't know what to do even if they did want to take action. That is where the book proposal comes in.

Q: What Can Go Wrong With a Book Proposal?

A: When a writer fails to define the need for the book or the market, the publisher may not be able to envision being able to sell the book. Other times, writers submit their proposal to the wrong person. So, do your research to make sure that you are sending it to an agent, publisher, or editor that works with the kind of material you are writing.

Q: Why Might I Be Turned Down?

A: The most common reason is not having a strong enough platform. Other reasons are that the book doesn't have a unique enough angle, or the marketplace is saturated with books that are too similar. Another issue is that the writer doesn't show that they have true expertise.

Q: Can I Write the Proposal After I Write the Book?

A: Yes. Sometimes, you need to just write the book and organize all the material before you have a full take on the material. You can write the proposal at any time that feels right for you.

Bite-Sized Thoughts for Chapter 4

1. You may have a lot of experience and feel you have a lot to say. But then you get to the blank page, and a clutching sensation creeps up. The first step is to just take a deep breath. (Do it!)

2. The next step is to explore with some fun, free-form brainstorming sessions. The first is: *The Junk Drawer Dump*. During this session, you will want to pour out anything and everything that you want to write about. No limits. The second brainstorming session: *What Do We Have Here?* is where you will begin to ask yourself if you see patterns or categories. See if the title might be emerging, or chapter titles. Notice if you are drawn to addressing a larger shift in thinking (Big Ideas), storytelling, reflections or vignettes (Stories), or a system (Plan-of-Action).

3. Allow the ideas time to percolate in your subconscious. Go for a walk, take a drive, play golf, make a pie. Get your hands busy and your mind off "figuring it all out." You'd be surprised what will bubble up to the surface when you let go and release the need to control the process.

4. Find a sounding board. If you find yourself going in circles within your mind, it may be time to talk to a friend or a person in your writing group, or hire a developmental editor or a writing coach. Even one session with a skilled professional can help cut through the noise and point you in a clear direction.

5. A book proposal is a valuable tool that can prompt you to think through and organize your ideas. It will help you to more fully understand why your book is a salable product in the current marketplace. It is either a tool to gain the interest of an agent or a business plan if you plan to self-publish. You can write your book proposal at any stage of the writing process.

PART TWO

LEARN THE CRAFT

CHAPTER 5

FINDING HOMES FOR YOUR IDEAS

"Help me! My ideas are homeless!"

I was working with Nina, a bright writer and high-concept thinker, on her book about language in the workplace. She was an accomplished speaker and a well-respected businesswoman. At our first meeting, we met for coffee to casually talk over her dreams and goals. She said she was having a hard time focusing. I asked her if she had tried brainstorming. Well, this question set her off. She told me that all she could do was brainstorm, but she didn't know what to do with all her hundreds of pages of brainstorming. About twenty minutes into the conversation, she just stopped talking. It was as if she was shutting down.

"What's going on?" I asked.

"It's just, I've been thinking about this book for ten years," she confessed. Then she pulled out five spiral notebooks.

"This is me, brainstorming. And I have ten more of these at home." She handed over the notebooks and continued. "I have all these ideas. It's like, way too many ideas, and I want to think that I can effectively communicate them to a reader, but they seem so free-form and lost."

"Your ideas seem lost?"

"Yeah, the image in my head is of my ideas as homeless, just wandering around looking for shelter!"

Nina's image stuck in my head. She had notebooks full of brainstorming sessions, but she had no idea how to translate all that brainstorming into synthesized, focused ideas. As we tossed around what was truly essential for her how-to book, the Three-Key Method was born.

Ready to dive in? Let's go!

Introduction to the Three-Key Method

Imagine that there is a magic door. This door unlocks the shape and style of your book. But to unlock this door, you need not one key, but three keys.

The Three Keys

Key #1: PROMISE. The promise is your WHY. Why is this a book your reader should buy? How does your book answer a clear need? What benefit will the reader receive by reading the book? How will your book provide a clear answer for your reader's concerns?

Key #2: PREMISE. The premise is your core idea, and your theme. It is the WHAT of your book. What is your book about? How is your core idea timely, educational, or inspirational? Can you home in on a theme that speaks to our collective humanity? Can you state your core idea in one to three sentences?

Key #3: APPROACH. The approach is the HOW. How are you going to present your material? What is the star of your show: Big Ideas, Stories, or a Plan-of-Action? How is your approach to the material fresh or unique? How might you describe your writing voice?

In this chapter you will find the Three-Key Method Worksheet, which will help you think through each of the Three Keys and find the answers that feel the most authentic and dynamic for you.

Breaking Down the Method: A Bachelorette, a Biker, and an Old Russian Walk Into a Hot Tub

About a year after my father died, I decided to go to the desert alone on some sort of pilgrimage. I thought I would get some solid time to work on this book, and if I needed to cry, I would allow myself to cry. I wound up at this seriously out-of-the-way desert-hot-springs hotel. This place was filled with characters. Apparently, it was a local hot spot for many Russians, and it was clear they ran the place. It was also a biker haven. Or, at least it was that weekend. On another note, on the first day I discovered what the thick musty heat did to my hair. My hair is prone to frizz anyway, but let's just say that the desert-hot-springs heat made my hair its own frizzball entity.

Late on the second night, I decided to take a soak in one of the hottest hot-spring tubs. It was there that I met a bachelorette, a biker, and an old Russian. I was brain-dead from a day of working on the book and fighting with my unruly hair. I wanted to melt into the water unseen. Unfortunately for me and my invisibility plans, the hot-springs hotel was one of the chattiest places on earth. The forty-year-old muscular biker chick leaned in.

"What are you? You look like a creative type."

"Was it the hair that gave me away?"

"I dunno, you just have that look. So, what are you?

I told them I was a writer, and that I was working on a book for female thought leaders. It was then that the Russian lady (think late sixties, bright red hair, and ready for a fight should one have arrived) chimed in.

"My grandfather was a writer. What a dick."

Then the happy-drunk young bachelorette leaned in. "So, you are, like, writing a book about writing a book?"

"Um, yeah, that's about right."

"Sounds redundant. What part are you on?" asked the Russian.

"I'm at the part where I teach people how to identify the three main components they will need to craft their book. I call it the Three-Key Method."

"I don't get it, you gotta say it better than that 'cause I don't get it," said the biker chick.

"Yeah and speak in layman's terms because I've had a lot of mojitos. Which, I love. I love mojitos," said the bachelorette.

At that point, a discussion ensued about how the drunken bachelorette shouldn't even be in the hot tub drunk, let alone the hottest hot tub, followed by a longer conversation about who makes the best mojitos in the area. I thought to myself, *ah, success; I can sit here now and be perfectly invisible.* The last thing I wanted to do was talk about my book. I thought maybe they would forget. But the demanding trio persisted. What was this Three-Key Method, and could I explain it fast and be clear because they were impatient and/or drunk. I remember thinking, *damn, this group may be my toughest audience; if I can explain it to them, I can explain it to anyone.*

I turned to the Russian (I never got anyone's names) and said, "Okay, so tell me what you want. Like right now, in your life."

"Right now, like right now? Like a glass of water?"

"Okay, maybe not *right* now, but, generally, in your life. What do you want?"

She thought. "I want a third career I don't hate, 'cause retirement sucks."

"Okay," I said. "So right now, there is a female thought leader writing a book about how to find the perfect job when you want to come out of retirement. She needs to convey three things to you, and she's got to do it quick."

The Russian's eyes got wide. I had her attention. "First, she has to tell you why you should read her book. She needs to make you a promise, and that is, yes, you can have a third happy career. That is Key #1.

"Next, for Key #2, she must tell you what the book will be about. She tells you she is going to discuss how to illuminate all your marketable skill sets, decide on the ones that are the most enjoyable, and help you to combine them to create a job that moves at the pace that you want to move.

"Then, she must write this book in a way that is fun or interesting to read, which is Key #3, or the approach. Her book is going to teach you how to create the job of your dreams, by taking you through a step-by-step system and supporting each step with entertaining stories along the way about how other people created their dream jobs."

The biker nodded, and the bachelorette screamed, "I love it!" (Though, in fairness, she loved everything that night.)

The Russian said thoughtfully, "I want to read that book."

Okay, so now it's your turn. In the following pages, I am going to walk you through each of the Three Keys, asking you specific questions that will help you to hone, delineate, and express the essence of your book with clarity and confidence.

Ready, Freddy?

The Three-Key Method Worksheet

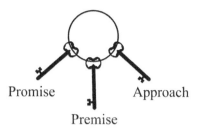

Promise   Approach

Premise

Promise

Who is my reader? _____

_____

_____

What is my reader's clear need? _____

_____

_____

How does my book offer an answer to their clear need? _____

_____

_____

Premise

How is my core idea timely, educational, or inspirational? ____

_____

_____

_____

How does my core idea speak to our collective humanity? ____

_____

_____

_____

How can I sum up my core idea in one to three sentences? ___

_____

_____

_____

_____

_____

Approach

Who is the star of my show: Big Ideas, Stories, or a Plan-of-Action?

_____

_____

_____

How is my approach to the material fresh or unique? _____

_____

_____

_____

_____

_____

How might I describe my unique writing voice? _____

_____

_____

_____

_____

Bite-Sized Thoughts for Chapter 5

1. The Three-Key Method will help you to think through not only the core concepts in your book but also the way you want to present those concepts to your reader.

2. **Key #1 is the PROMISE.** The promise is your WHY. Why should the reader buy this book? How will it help the reader or answer a clear need? What benefit will the reader receive by reading the book?

3. **Key #2 is the PREMISE**, or your core idea. It is the WHAT of your book. What is your book about? Is your core idea timely, educational, or inspirational? Can you state your core idea in one to four sentences?

4. **Key #3 is the APPROACH.** The approach is the HOW. How are you going to present your material in a way that is fresh or unique? How might you describe your writing voice? What is the star of your show: your Big Ideas, your Stories, or a Plan-of-Action?

5. Be patient. What you are unearthing are the core concepts of your book, the pillars upon which everything else is built. By completing the Three-Key Method worksheet, you might realize that you have some clarity and some cloudiness. This is normal. Don't worry about having all the answers right away. In the next three chapters, you will get to dive a little deeper and explore your promise, your premise, and your approach.

CHAPTER 6

KEY #1: PROMISE

Your Book Must Make a Clear and Compelling PROMISE

The promise is your WHY. Why should the reader buy your book? The promise is your pitch to the reader, explaining how your book will help or answer a clear need. The promise identifies the benefit or benefits that the reader will experience after reading your book. Remember that your reader has a problem or question in their life. Your promise is that your book holds that answer, and it will be clear (and not confusing). Spending time reading your book will, in some way, make their life better.

In this chapter, we will cover three questions that will help you to think through your promise. Then, I will provide you with a real-life example, showing you how a writer just like you thought through her promise. Next we will take a look at how three bestselling books—*The Life-Changing Magic of Tidying Up: The Japanese Art of Decluttering and Organizing* by Marie Kondo; *Playing Big: Practical Wisdom for Women Who Want to Speak Up, Create, and Lead* by Tara Mohr; and *Thrive: The Third Metric to Redefining Success and Creating a Life of Well-Being, Wisdom, and Wonder* by Arianna Huffington—answered the Promise Questions.

Defining the Need

Years ago, I was a young and stupid therapist-in-training. In one of my Intro-to-Therapy classes, my wise instructor asked the group of students, "When do you think most people pick up the phone and make an appointment for therapy?"

Silence. Then a few hands went up.

"When they feel like they could use some new skills to make their life better," one student said. The instructor grimaced. That wasn't it. Another hand went up.

"When they want to know if they have a diagnosis?" Nope. There was silence. We had nothing.

The instructor leaned in for emphasis. "By far, most people call to make an appointment for therapy when they are in crisis."

He went on to explain why. In that moment, they have a clear need. They feel they can no longer answer their own questions, and they need an outside source to provide hope, information, options, or another perspective.

I have come to learn that it is basically the same for self-help books. When do most people shell out their hard-earned money for a self-help book? When they are in crisis or have a clear need. They have a question in their mind that they alone cannot answer.

The Three Promise Questions

To flesh out your core idea, let's first look at the three Promise Questions.

1. **Who is your reader?**
    Who are the people that will pick up your book? Women? Men? Teens? Business-minded professionals? Aspiring

gourmet cooks? Try to narrow your focus here. You don't need to be overly specific, but don't be too broad, either.

2. **What is your reader's clear need?**
   What issue is urging your reader to pick up your book? What questions or problems do they have? Remember, your reader is struggling with something. Business stagnation, finances, romance, work, dating, emotions, a poor attitude, unwanted behaviors, stress, anxiety, depression, marriage, health, aging, clutter, housework, diet, friendships, family, pain, grief, lack of a specific skill set, etc. You can use the "Needs of My Readers" chart on page 98 to help you identify the needs you will be addressing.

3. **How does your book answer their clear need?**
   You should be able to articulate how your book is a direct response to their questions or problems.

What helped me to better understand the needs of my own readers was to study the work of Abraham Maslow. Maslow was an American psychologist who, after studying the needs of human beings, created what is known as Maslow's Hierarchy of Needs. It's a theory of psychological health. It illustrates that first we have survival/basic needs like food, water, and shelter. If those basic human needs are met, we can move up the pyramid, and up and up, until we are working toward self-actualization, or reaching our full potential.

Self-Actualization → reaching your full potential
Esteem → needs of the ego, status
Love, belonging → how we connect to others
Safety → a sense of security, feeling safe from harm
Survival → having your basic needs met like
food, water and shelter

If you look at Maslow's Hierarchy of Needs you will see that we all, in some way, have the same needs and desires.

Heavily inspired by Maslow's hierarchy (full props, Maslow), I invite you to look over the "Needs of My Readers" chart.

What Are the Needs of My Readers?

Love & Connection
Community or Intimacy

Self-Realization
Creativity, Full Potential

Giving Back
Thinking Beyond the Self

Accomplishment
Achievement, Acknowledgment

Physical Health
Expression, Connection

Spiritual Fulfillment
Practice, Connection

Mental Health
Stability, Tools

Safety
Security from Threats

Bodily Needs
Food, Water, Warmth

Sally and Jenna's Story

Let's explore the idea of the PROMISE by looking at a real-life example, the story of Sally and Jenna.

Jenna is a thirty-seven-year-old corporate businesswoman, wife, and mom of three. She is sick and tired of working at a job she doesn't like and that takes her away from her family. Jenna wants to start her own online business.

Sally is a fifty-year-old mom of four. When she was thirty-five, she too felt just like Jenna. She hated her corporate job, saw that promotion was highly limited, and didn't like the long hours away from her family. She started an online business, and she worked it until it was making enough of a profit that she could quit her day job. Sally's friends saw what she had done, and they asked if Sally could help them to do the same. She did. Sally was so effective at providing guidance that other women sought her out. She started a small consulting career.

After a decade of trial and error, Sally came up with a streamlined method that helped women transition from careers for which they had no passion or interest into online businesses that offered them a sense of personal control and purpose. Sally began to write about her method of career transformation for magazines and blogs. She even won some awards for her work. Sally felt that her tools were not common knowledge, and she decided to write a book that detailed how any woman can create a thriving online business that they love.

Jenna lived in a different state in a rural area and didn't know anyone who had ever started his or her own business. It simply wasn't something that anyone in her circle of friends had ever done. She felt a little depressed, and was not sure how to make the transition.

What did Jenna need? Sally's book.

What did Sally need? To write the book.

How Sally Answered the Promise Questions

1. **Who is your reader?**
   At first, Sally was nervous about pinpointing her audience. She knew that most of the women she worked with were around the ages of thirty to fifty-five and had kids. Some were married, some were divorced, and some were single. She was concerned that if she targeted her book to women her age then she might miss the younger demographic who were also interested in creating online businesses.

   Sally's answer: Women (professional, struggling) who are ready for a transition toward becoming their own boss and creating an online business.

2. **What is your reader's clear need?**
   This part was easy for Sally. She had spoken to thousands of women who were looking to make a transition.

   Sally's answer: My readers need some encouragement to help them face all the fears that may come up during the process. They want to know how their skill sets will translate, and if they need to learn new skill sets. My readers need specific and clear tools to leave their workaday world and move into ownership of an online business. My readers need to know how to network and promote to expand their business to keep it sustainable.

3. **How does your book answer their clear need?**
   Sally had answers; she just hadn't organized all her thoughts. It took her a week to think through this one.

   Sally's answer: My book looks at the common fears that women have about becoming their own bosses, leaving a "steady" job, and defining their own careers. My book offers clear tools that will teach the readers how to determine if their product or service is viable, define their target customer, effectively market their product, and keep the business growing.

What Sally Did Next

By answering the questions, Sally realized she had found a structure for her book. She decided that her book would be broken up into three parts and would examine the emotional preparedness (the fears of her readers), offer specific tools to launch, and provide clear guidance to keep it sustainable. She saw that she was writing a book that offered a clear plan-of-action. She thought of it this way

> Part One: **Make It Happen** (No Matter What Fears You May Have)
>
> Part Two: **Make It Work** (And Here's How: Eleven Steps to Your Online Business)
>
> Part Three: **Make It Last** (Seven Specific Ways to Network, Promote, and Grow Your Business)

Three Promise Questions: Examples From the Bookshelf

Utilizing the three Promise Questions, let's examine a few examples from popular or bestselling books.

Again, the Promise Questions Are

1. Who is your reader?
2. What is your reader's clear need?
3. How does my book answer their clear need?

EXAMPLE 1

The Life-Changing Magic of Tidying Up:
The Japanese Art of Decluttering and Organizing
by Marie Kondo

The Typical Reader: An American woman (or man, but mostly, woman) who is a consumer and is organizationally challenged. She consumes products on a regular basis and has little-to-no working system of organization.

The Clear Need: Their house is disorganized and cluttered. They have a lot of stuff and don't know what to do with it. They are not sure what to keep and what to throw away. They have no system, or a system that is not working.

The Clear Answer: Learn the KonMari method of tidying up from Japanese cleaning expert, Marie Kondo. You will be able to organize your house swiftly and painlessly. Kondo's method will teach you how an organized house provides greater access to lightness, allows you to let go of the weight of things you never needed, and to simplify, organize, and store your possessions in a way that leads to daily joy.

The Promise in a Nutshell: There is an effortless way to get organized and let go of items you really don't need and to feel joy in the process.

EXAMPLE 2

Playing Big: Practical Wisdom for Women
Who Want to Speak Up, Create, and Lead
by Tara Mohr

The Typical Reader: Career-age women who are holding themselves back and not meeting their full potential.

The Clear Need: They have big dreams or ideas, but they are afraid of taking action. They are not sure if they are worthy of playing bigger in the world.

The Clear Answer: Tara Mohr, leadership coach, will reveal her proven, innovative tools that will teach you the practical, hands-on strategies you will need to speak up, pursue your dreams, and lead the boundless life you want to be living.

The Promise in a Nutshell: Whether you are an entrepreneur, activist, or a professional in a corporation, you can find the inner strength, learn the practical tools, and play as big as you want in this world.

EXAMPLE 3

Thrive: The Third Metric to Redefining Success and
Creating a Life of Well-Being, Wisdom, and Wonder
by Arianna Huffington

The Typical Reader: Overworked people who are trying to "do it all," all the time, and who have sought out money and power as their prizes in life and feel overwhelmed or exhausted. Most likely women ages thirty to sixty.

The Clear Need: They are exhausted from the unending treadmill experience where all they do is try to earn more and more, working harder and faster than everyone else. They are not happy or fulfilled. They are burned-out and stressed-out.

The Clear Answer: There is a third metric for measuring success beyond the pursuit of money and power, and that is living a rich and fulfilling life. Arianna Huffington, the wildly successful businesswoman, can show you how to make a shift from climbing the ladder to creating a life filled with unplugging, mindfulness, giving, and cherished moments. If you follow this third metric, your life will be calmer and happier.

The Promise in a Nutshell: If you follow Arianna's lead and adopt this third metric, you will not only succeed but you will thrive.

Key #1: Promise Worksheet

Who is your reader? _____

_____

_____

_____

What is your reader's clear need? _____

_____

_____

_____

How does your book answer your reader's clear need? _____

_____

_____

_____

Bite-Sized Thoughts for Chapter 6

1. The first key in the Three-Key Method is the promise. The promise answers the question, *why should the reader buy your book?* The promise identifies the benefit or benefits that the reader will experience after reading your book.

2. To fulfill the promise, you must know your reader. Take a moment to ask, *who is my reader? Who is the typical person that will want to purchase my book?*

3. The second part of knowing your reader is to be able to answer, *what is my reader's clear need?*

4. The third aspect is knowing the connection point between your reader and your book. In other words, *how does my book offer an answer to my reader's need?*

5. Spend some time with your favorite books. Ask yourself, *what is the promise of this book and why did I purchase it? What clear need did I have and how did this book answer that particular need?*

CHAPTER 7

KEY #2: PREMISE

Old Jews and the Best Pastrami Sandwich in New York

I love old Jews. They drive me crazy, but I love them. Mostly they drive me crazy because when I teach them, they can go wildly off track and take the class on wacky (but interesting) diversions. (Also, I plan to be an old Jew one day.) Bottom line, it can be hard to pull old Jews back into focus. They tend to be feisty.

Okay, so let me set the stage for you. I was teaching a class on nonfiction writing for a Creative Aging Class, and to put it bluntly, I was going down fast. I had been trying for ten minutes to explain what I meant by "the premise" of a book, and nothing I was saying seemed to be clicking.

Wanda, a woman with wild orange lips, chimed in, "This is getting too complicated." Another yawning woman, Norma, told me that I talked too much. A third told me that she didn't really want to be in this class, but she needed to kill some time before Quilting with Clara started. A fourth said that he was old and that if I didn't get to the point quickly he might not make it.

They chatted amongst themselves, wondering what the quilting class would be like that day. I tried to offer an example, but I was flailing. The room was noisy, I was getting anxious, and it just wasn't pretty.

That's when this awesome man in his late seventies (let's call him Morris) came to my rescue.

"She's talking about the best pastrami sandwich, at Katz's Deli!" he said. Suddenly, everyone got quiet. Morris had the floor. "Look," he said. "There are plenty of places to get a good-enough pastrami sandwich in New York, am I right?" Several nodded. "Most everyone can do the bread okay, the pickles maybe, but the meat, *the pastrami*, that's another thing. Do you know that at Katz's they cure that meat for up to four weeks, then they smoke it in a spice rub, and then they boil it? Very long process." It was around this time that I got nervous. Were we just traveling down the rabbit hole of pastrami making? But Morris continued.

"During the summer of 1964, my Uncle Teddy and I spent three months trying every deli from Buffalo to Poughkeepsie, searching for the best pastrami sandwich. We took the subway for hours, trekked up hills, and made our way into tiny hole-in-the-wall delis in Hoboken. We're talking Artie's, Ben's, Moishe's, Second Avenue, Carnegie, Gottlieb's, Frankel's. It took us months, but we were determined. And hands down, the best pastrami sandwich was at Katz's Deli in New York City."

Everyone nodded. Wanda, unfazed, balked. "What the hell does this have to do with writing a book? With this premise thing?"

"Do I have to spell it out?"

"Yes, yes, you have to spell it out," Wanda demanded.

Morris's voice was clear and crisp. "Anyone can grab two slices of bread, throw some average pastrami inside, and call it a pastrami sandwich. But the quality of the meat is what makes the difference. This premise thing this crazy girl is talking about, **that is the meat**. Crappy meat, crappy sandwich. Crappy premise, crappy book."

Morris paused for dramatic effect. "You see, almost everyone can make a sandwich, but not everyone can make a Katz's pastrami sandwich. It's the meat. She's talking about the meat!"

The entire group nodded, some mumbling, "Ah, the meat."

"Okay, well fine," Wanda said. "That's all you had to say."

With that, everyone seemed to understand the idea of a premise and we happily moved on. After the class, I thanked Morris for his help. I told him that the story about his Uncle Teddy was great, and that maybe he should write it down, it was so good.

"Yeah, I made that uncle stuff up. You were dying out there."

I stifled a laugh as he walked off. Then he turned around. "But the Katz's Deli part is real; their pastrami is heaven." And then he walked off without a goodbye.

Note: In doing research for the book, I indeed found out that Katz's Deli is often considered the best pastrami sandwich in New York.

The Three Premise Questions

So, the premise is the core idea, the WHAT, or the meat of the sandwich.

It's really what we, the readers, are here for.

1. How is your core idea timely, educational, or inspirational?
2. How does your core idea speak to our collective humanity?

3. How can you sum up your core idea in one to four sentences?

Timely, Educational, or Inspirational

The core idea of your book should be timely. People should be (more or less) ready to hear this message, usually because there is a clear need at this particular moment. (But if you are ahead of your time, I say put it out there anyway; let everyone else catch up!)

The core idea is often educational. Your reader has picked up the book not simply to be entertained, but to learn something specific.

The core idea is often inspirational. It may provide a sense of hope and optimism. It inspires the reader to think, believe, or behave differently.

Q: Does the Core Idea Have to Be All Three (Timely, Educational, and Inspirational)?

A: No, but the most effective and bestselling books often have all three.

Speaking to Our Collective Humanity

The strongest thought leader books tap into our common struggles, desires, and hopes as human beings. Thought leaders are able to read trends and sense the current state of our human experience. (What's working, what's not.)

Though you may have a niche market, you will still be speaking to our collective humanity.

Q: How Do I Know If My Book Is Speaking to Our Collective Humanity?

A: Turn back to page 98. If your book touches upon one or more needs on the "Needs of My Readers" Chart, you are good to go.

Summing It Up

Ah, this is where most good ideas go to die. A good idea should be easy to articulate, yet many writers struggle when it comes time to sum it up in a few concise sentences. They find they can talk about their book for an hour, but they can't communicate their core idea. So, what happens? They tend to ramble or confuse the listener. And if you ramble in your idea, chances are that your book will ramble. Clarity is key.

Be patient with this part of the process. Summing it up seems like it should be easy, yet often writers describe it as harder than writing their entire book. If you struggle in this area, do not dismay. I am about to teach you a quick and dirty formula that will help you to effectively articulate your idea. (And it's virtually painless.)

Hint: No need to be flowery here. The goal here is clear communication. We want to understand your book idea in one to four sentences.

Guide to Summing Up Your Idea

What are my ELECTRIC WORDS?

Electric words = key words that are *the most essential* to define your idea. They are electric because they contain a certain accurate and exciting energy when brought together. You will find these words in the titles of the book or on the back cover used to describe the book.

Examples of some electric words and phrases used by female thought leaders:

Women, research, evidence-based, statistics, growing trend, lasting change, improve lives, increase knowledge base, revolutionary approach, competitive advantage, executive, nonprofit, expert, groundbreaking, practical tools, community, cultural awareness, health-conscious, spiritual, true-life stories, etc.

Free Associate: What electric words belong in your short pitch?

_____

_____

_____

_____

_____

_____

_____

The Sum-It-Up Formula

Next, use the Sum-It-Up formula to help you think through the information needed to help you shape your short pitch.

What → *Who* → *Goal* → *Result*

What	→	Title of your book
Who	→	Your reader (audience)
Goal	→	What your reader will learn
Result	→	How your reader's life will change as a result

The Sum-It-Up Formula: Examples From the Bookshelf

Women Rocking Business: The Ultimate Step-by-Step Guidebook to Create a Thriving Life Doing Work You Love by Sage Lavine

What: *Women Rocking Business*

Who: Women ready to bring powerful feminine values such as generosity, spiritual fulfillment, and social and environmental awareness to the business realm.

Goal: To teach women how to identify their gift to the world, heal their relationship with money, and offer groundbreaking tools on marketing, sales, and service.

Result: To create a successful, sustainable business that is also spiritually fulfilling.

Summing It Up: *Women Rocking Business* by Sage Lavine is for all women who are ready to bring their unique feminine values to the realm of business. Sage will teach you how to identify your gift to the world, heal your relationship with money, and introduce you to some essential tools of marketing, sales, and service to create a business that is successful, spiritually fulfilling, and sustainable.

Patty and Donna's Story

Patty was a funny, bold salesperson moving up in her company. But she was hitting a major roadblock. Every time she came up for a promotion, she would receive the same feedback.

"Your communication style is too blunt. Too direct. Soften it up a bit."

This feedback confused Patty, because it was exactly those blunt, honest, and quirky communication skills that tended to work with her American clients. However, whenever she dealt with potential clients from China, India, or the Middle East, she came up short.

Donna was a communication trainer for major corporations. She had noticed a few years back that communication differences were getting in the way of her clients making sales overseas. She tried to explain the cultural differences in communication styles but found that often, she was unable to do so. After a few years of struggling, she came up with a metric to explain the communication differences, so that the various cultures could better understand one another.

Donna noticed a trend, that more and more companies were going global and they were coming up against the same roadblocks. Soon, she found that she had more work than she could handle. She needed a workbook for her training sessions, something she could leave behind for the participants to review. She began writing, and as the pages added up, she realized she had the basis for an insightful book on international communication styles. She thought she would call it *Speak Everyone's Language*.

Meanwhile, Patty came up for another promotion, and received another denial. Her company informed her what she could not do, but didn't offer any education so she could learn a new skill set.

What did Patty need?

Donna's book.

How Donna Answered the Premise Questions

Premise Question #1: How is your core idea timely, educational, or inspirational?

Donna's Answer: The book was so timely that Donna feared that if she didn't publish it quickly, another book answering the need might come out. Her book was also educational, because it provided direct tools that were easy to understand and implement.

Initially, her book was not inspirational. But the more she thought about it, the more she realized it could be. She realized that she would often have to inspire her clients by showing them the potential for growth if they followed her system. Donna decided to bring an inspirational tone to her writing.

Premise Question #2: How does your core idea speak to our collective humanity?

Donna's Answer: Donna looked over the "Needs of My Readers" chart and noticed that her system would fulfill three needs. Her system impacted their basic needs because it helped them bring home a paycheck that would cover basic sustenance. It impacted their psychological needs because many experienced a boost in self-esteem when they successfully created relationships with clients overseas and improved their sense of self-accomplishment at work. It impacted their self-actualization needs because for some, learning to communicate across cultures offered an opportunity to reach their full potential in a work setting.

Premise Question #3: How can you sum up your idea in one to four sentences?

Donna's Answer: Donna struggled with this one. How to take all her years of research and expertise and finesse it into four sentences?

First, she brainstormed her electric words:

Communication, international, closing deals, guide, American, business, sales, increase

Then she used the *what, who, goal, result* formula to help her think through her answer.

What: Her book, *Speak Everyone's Language*

Who: The American businessperson in need of communication tools when dealing with international clients.

Goal: Learn how to communicate and close deals with clients from differing cultures.

Result: New skill set that could lead to increased sales, boost in company morale, and general company expansion.

Summing It Up: *Speak Everyone's Language* will teach you, the American businessperson, to better understand and communicate with your international clients. You will be guided through specific and effective communication tools that will empower you to close any deal in any land.

The Three Premise Questions: Examples From the Bookshelf

Now considering the three questions, let's go back to the bookshelf and look at some examples of books in the current marketplace. The three books we will be looking at are *Quiet: The Power of Introverts in a World That Can't Stop Talking* by Susan Cain, *Secrets of Six-Figure Women: Surprising Strategies to Up Your*

Earnings and Change Your Life by Barbara Stanny, and *Big Magic: Creative Living Beyond Fear* by Elizabeth Gilbert.

Here Are the Premise Questions Once More

1. How is your core idea timely, educational, or inspirational?
2. How does your core idea speak to our collective humanity?
3. How can you sum up your core idea in one to four sentences?

EXAMPLE 1

*Quiet: The Power of Introverts in a World
That Can't Stop Talking*
by Susan Cain

How is the core idea timely?

We live in a loud world. A world where many are clamoring for attention on social media, television, and online. Cain's book reaches out to the introverts who may possess great talents but not be comfortable with self-promotion.

How is the core idea educational?

Cain is teaching introverts how they can tap into their quiet power, utilizing their listening skills and creativity to express themselves more fully. The book also teaches extroverts how they can stop underestimating the introverts in their life.

How is the core idea inspirational?

The author writes about successful introverts including salesmen and public speakers, letting us know that nothing is off the table if you are an introvert.

How does this book home in on a theme that speaks to our collective humanity?

The theme here is that we all can have a voice, though some may be more outwardly expressive than others. Cain speaks to our need to be fully realized human beings.

How can you sum up your core idea into a compelling hook?

What: *Quiet: The Power of Introverts in a World that Can't Stop Talking*

Who: Introverts who, though they have talents, may feel that they will be left behind or undervalued in a culture that applauds the self-promoting extrovert.

Goal: Through powerful stories and remarkable research, and with passionate arguments, Susan Cain persuades us that the time has come to change the way we see introverts.

Result: If we are the introvert, Susan Cain shows us that we are not alone and that we can be wickedly effective and highly impactful. If we are the extrovert, Susan Cain will teach us that it's time to stop underestimating the introvert and to recognize them for the powerhouses that they truly are.

Summing It Up: *Quiet: The Power of Introverts in a World that Can't Stop Talking* is an important book for introverts who, though they have talents, feel that they are undervalued in a culture that applauds the self-promoting extrovert. Through powerful stories and remarkable research, and with passionate arguments, Susan Cain persuades us that the time has come to change the way we see introverts. If we are the introvert, Susan Cain shows us that we are not alone, and that we can be highly effective and impactful. If we are the extrovert, Susan Cain teaches us that it is time to stop underestimating the introvert, and to recognize them for the powerhouses they truly are.

EXAMPLE 2

Secrets of Six-Figure Women:
Surprising Strategies to Up Your Earnings and Change Your Life
by Barbara Stanny

How is the core idea timely?

There is still high gender inequality when it comes to pay. For every dollar a man makes, a woman only makes between 50 and 80 cents. Yet at the same time, the number of women who are pulling in six figures or more is swiftly increasing. Stanny is right there to help stoke the fires of this upward trend, offering secrets and tools to help women earn what they are worth.

How is the core idea educational?

Stanny interviewed a host of women making six figures and above. Her research revealed surprising results; though these women came from all walks of life and industries and a myriad of backgrounds, there were threads of commonality. They all possessed certain characteristics. Stanny offers her research to help women review their old scars and disparaging views about money and to learn how to stretch their visions to achieve financial abundance.

How is the core idea inspirational?

Stanny offers her readers a clear "You can do this" attitude. She offers inspiration to push beyond fear and self-imposed limits to reach higher and be more effective when it comes to earning money. It's no surprise that Stanny is also a motivational speaker.

How does this book home in on a theme that speaks to our collective humanity?

Stanny speaks to our basic needs, our sense of accomplishment, our balanced mental health, our need for stability, and our desire to be fully realized human beings.

How can you sum up your core idea swiftly and cleanly?

What: *Secrets of Six-Figure Women: Surprising Strategies to Up Your Earning and Change Your Life*

Who: Women from every industry who may be working hard but not making what they are worth. Women who want to better understand what it takes to make a six-figure salary.

Goal: To offer practical tips, tools, and inspiration to help women earn more money.

Result: Women who are ready to show up and move upward faster can glean tools and insights that will help them ensure their wealth.

Summing It Up: *Secrets of Six-Figure Women: Surprising Strategies to Up Your Earnings and Change Your Life* is for any woman who may be hardworking, yet not seeing the effects in her bank account. Stanny offers insight to help women understand what might be holding them back, as well as tips, tools, and inspiration to help them realize an abundant financial future.

EXAMPLE 3

Big Magic: Creative Living Beyond Fear
by Elizabeth Gilbert

How is the core idea timely?

Right now, in our culture we are exploring the idea of hiding our best selves, of challenging the idea of being small or playing small. *Big Magic* speaks to the many people who are ready to play big, spread their wings creatively, and believe in magic, maybe the way they once did as a child.

How is the core idea educational?

Gilbert offers funny and conversational advice on how to break out of ruts, face your fears, and live a more productive creative life. Gilbert reveals her own struggles, to show the reader that you can learn how to view the creative process with curiosity over fear, and, eventually, uncover your unique creative path.

How is the core idea inspirational?

She shares the practices of great artists in order to demystify the creative process and encourage daily inspiration.

How does this book home in on a theme that speaks to our collective humanity?

This book speaks to the people who are addressing their needs of self-expression, accomplishment, and self-actualization.

How can you sum up your core idea swiftly and cleanly?

What: *Big Magic: Creative Living Beyond Fear*

Who: Creative thinkers, including aspiring writers and artists who tend to shut down their best, most creative selves. For those who struggle to produce work despite a deep desire to create.

Goal: To demystify the creative process. Gilbert will teach you how to pursue a creative life driven by curiosity over fear. In a funny, conversational tone, she shares her own stories and the practices of great artists, to show you how to access your most creative self.

Result: Reading Gilbert's book will show you how to face old patterns and break out of ruts, and it illuminates how to experience daily enthusiasm and inspiration. Gilbert will help you to unleash the creative magic within.

Summing It Up: *Big Magic: Creative Living Beyond Fear* is for all creative thinkers who tend to shut down their best, most creative selves. In a funny, conversational tone, Gilbert shares her own stories as well as the practices of great artists, in order to demystify the creative process. Reading Gilbert's book will help you to face old patterns and break out of unproductive ruts. By showing you how to pursue a creative life driven by curiosity over fear, Gilbert will help you to unleash the big creative magic within.

Key #2: Premise Worksheet

How is your premise timely? _____

_____

How is your premise educational? _____

_____

How is your premise inspirational? _____

_____

How does your premise speak to our collective humanity? ____

_____

_____

What are your electric words? _____

_____

_____

How can you sum up your core idea swiftly and cleanly? (If not, see the Sum-It-Up formula below) _____

_____

_____

What → Title of your book _____

_____

Who → Your reader (audience) _____

_____

Goal → What your audience will learn _____

_____

_____

Result → How your reader's life will change as a result _____

_____

_____

_____

_____

Bite-Sized Thoughts for Chapter 7

1. The second key in the Three-Key Method is the premise. Think of the premise as the meat in a sandwich. It's the core idea; the true reason the reader purchases your book. It answers the question, *what is my book about?*

2. The first question that will help define your premise is, *how is my core idea timely, educational, or inspirational?*

3. The second question that will help define your premise is, *how does my core idea speak to our collective humanity?*

4. A core idea is most effective if you can communicate it clearly and succinctly. If you struggle to answer the third question, *how can I sum up my idea in one to four sentences?* use the Sum-It-Up formula:

   What   → Title of book
   Who   → Audience
   Goal   → What your audience will learn
   Result → How your reader's life will change as a result

5. Take a moment to review the books you have recently purchased. You probably browsed over some of them quickly and made a pretty fast decision. What electric words drew you to pick up the book? What does their one-to four-sentence pitch read like? Is it concise? Compelling? What, in the end, made you spend money on that book?

CHAPTER 8

KEY #3: APPROACH

The Fellow Traveler, the Guide, and the Wild Cheerleader

We all need mentors, coaches, and teachers to light the way. Chances are you have had a few that have changed your life. Think of the top three people who made an impact, paved a path, or opened a door for you. Ask, what was their communication style? How did they reach you? Were they kind and loving, outspoken and forceful, determined and feisty?

As I look back on the three people who have influenced me the most, I realize that they all had vastly different styles. My first mentor was Hesper Anderson. She was the screenwriter of the film, *Children of a Lesser God*. Her father was the famous playwright Maxwell Anderson, who wrote *The Bad Seed*. I met Hesper at the USC School of Filmic Writing, as it was called at the time, and she invited me to join her group of ragtag and boisterous writing colleagues. Hesper was gentle and open. She shared her struggles, her fears, her vulnerability. She allowed us to walk alongside her in the writing journey. She laughed with us, she cried with us. Hesper was a fellow traveler.

My next mentor was John Vorhaus. I first discovered John when I picked up his popular book, *The Comic Toolbox: How to Be Funny Even If You're Not*. At the time I cracked open the book, I was struggling as a writer. I kept getting feedback something akin to "good writer but it doesn't quite hold together." John's book shifted everything for me. He had a way of approaching writing with clear recipes and game-changing formulas. His words were practical, and his systems made sense. Later, when I met him in person, I found out what a lovable man he was as well. But truth be told, it was his "writing maps" that changed my life. John was a guide.

My last mentor was Judy Reeves. She is the author of *A Writers Book of Days: A Spirited Companion & Lively Muse for the Writing Life* and *Wild Women, Wild Voices: Writing From Your Authentic Wildness*. I met Judy right after my divorce, when I was a puddle of mush. I had just left a good job and a town I loved, and I had a nine-month-old baby on my hip. Judy ran the local writing organization, and the moment I met her, I felt welcomed. I quickly started taking every class Judy offered. I found she provided not only sage writing advice, but also a space to heal and grow. Since coming to know Judy, I have seen thousands of the lives she has touched, and we all feel the same way. She imparts her wisdom, roots for all of us to succeed, and encourages us to howl at the moon. Judy is a wild cheerleader.

You are now in the position to make an impact on someone's life.

What is your style, what is your approach?

Books Are Like Personalities

Some books are big, bold, and tell-it-like-it-is. Some are poetic and lyrical. Some get right to the point, while others take their time telling stories or jokes. Your book will have a personality all its own.

Key #3, the Approach, refers to how you are going to present the material to your reader; how you will organize it and communicate it, and how you hope to make the information stick. Your approach captures the personality of your book.

Let's Look Once Again at the Three Approach Questions

1. Who is the star of your show? Big Ideas, Stories, or a Plan-of-Action?

    (Here's where I introduce you to the Dynamic Thought Leader Templates.)

2. How is your book fresh or unique?

3. How would you describe your writer's voice?

Approach Question #1: Who is the star of my show? Choosing Your Template

Your book may contain aspects of all three templates. You will most likely be offering up some big ideas, some stories (or vignettes), and maybe a plan-of-action or two. Zeroing in on a template will help you to identify who is the star of your show (and who will be the background players).

Who is the star of your show?

- Use the Big Ideas Template if your overall approach is a call to action or a call for a general shift in thinking, or if you will be using a variety of tools to illuminate your ideas.
- Use the Stories Template if the bulk of your material is presented either in one big story or a collection of stories, vignettes, or reflections.
- Use the Plan-of-Action Template if you have a clear system to teach your reader.

The Templates in Action: Examples From the Bookshelf

To better understand how the templates work, let's take a look at a few examples from the bookshelf to see how successful authors utilized them.

EXAMPLE OF THE BIG IDEAS TEMPLATE

Lean In: Women, Work, and the Will to Lead
by Sheryl Sandberg

This book is a great example of the Big Ideas Template. Sandberg's overall goal is to spark a conversation about empowering women in the workplace. The book starts off with a dedication and introduction. The meat of the book consists of eleven chapters, which contain research, hard data, and personal anecdotes to bring her big ideas (surrounding a shift in thinking and culture) to light. Sandberg ends the book with a "let's keep talking" section, acknowledgments, notes, and an index.

EXAMPLE OF THE STORIES TEMPLATE

Chicken Soup for the Soul: Devotional Stories for Women:
101 Daily Devotions to Comfort, Encourage, and Inspire Women
by Susan M. Heim & Karen Talcott

This book is a wonderful example of the Stories Template. Heim and Talcott have gathered 101 devotional stories from female authors. The book begins with a forward by Jennifer Sands, whose husband Jim Sands was killed in Tower One of the World Trade Center on September 11, 2001. The introduction is written by both authors. The stories are organized under eleven topics: Faith, Motherhood, Life Lessons, Illness, God's Helpers, Parenting, Relationships, Loss, Service to Others, Marriage, and Self-Esteem. After each story is a short devotional prayer. The book concludes with sections titled: Meet Our Contributors, Meet Our Authors, Thank You, and About *Chicken Soup for the Soul.*

EXAMPLE OF THE PLAN-OF-ACTION TEMPLATE

Boss Bitch: A Simple 12-Step Plan to Take Charge of Your Career
by Nicole Lapin

This book is an excellent example of the Plan-of-Action Template. Lapin's goal is to take her reader through her savvy 12-Step plan toward claiming the career of her dreams. She starts off with a dedication (to her former self!), a table of contents, a quote, and an introduction. The meat of the book is an actionable guide that is broken up into three sections. Section one covers two steps, section two covers five steps, and section three covers the remaining five steps of her 12-Step Plan. Lapin uses personal anecdotes to bring the steps to life for her reader. The book ends with The Business Dictionary, acknowledgments, and an index.

Did you notice? → Even though the authors used different templates and approaches, they all used stories of some kind.

Approach Question #2: How is this book fresh or unique?

If you are providing information that has been covered before, your book will simply not go as far as it can, even if you are imparting valuable information. What readers are looking for is, *what is new about this approach?* One easy way to freshen up your approach is to—you guessed it— tell some stories.

Telling a Good Story Cures the Fresh/Unique Issue

If it's not in your wheelhouse, one of the most important skill sets you will want to work on is telling a good story. You can use these skills in your writing, when giving presentations, or in important deal-making conversations. Why? Stories bring your black-and-white ideas into full color for the reader. Stories make your ideas real, relatable, and understandable. Stories help people connect to the data on an emotional level.

Storytelling Works, and Here Is Why

1. Stories create instant focus. We tend to lose our focus often, especially in this modern, tech-heavy world. It's normal for our minds to wander and daydream. However, when a good story is being told, the meandering stops, and the brain focuses.

2. A bond is created between the writer and reader. Have you heard of neural coupling? It's what is happening when the brain of the listener connects to the storyteller. Mirror neurons create a coherence between the audience and the speaker.

3. Good stories engage us emotionally. Psychologists call this narrative transport. While reading a powerful story, the reader will have positive, engaged emotions. When reading a compelling or emotional story, the brain chemistry changes as the brain produces oxytocin, which is often

known to increase compassion, generosity, trustworthiness, and sensitivity.

4. Stories literally "light us up." Functional MRI studies show that the brain reacts differently to stories than it does to facts. When the brain hears facts, two regions activate. Hearing stories causes several additional areas to light up. The brain is responding as if the story were happening to the reader.

5. Stories make facts more memorable. The brain remembers facts more easily when told in story form. Stories enhance memory.

According to research by psychologists Melanie C. Green and Timothy Brock, stories hold quite an influence over the mind. Green and Brock believe that people often underestimate just how much stories make an impact on them. Stories can take us on a journey, transport us to another time and place, help us to consider new information, and question ideas we may not normally question.

Three Creative Ways to Use Storytelling

The Overall Case Study

Some writers take a case example or several case examples and follow them throughout their book. This is an interesting approach because the reader becomes bonded to the person (or people) in the case study, and will wonder what will happen to them, much like they would if they were reading a novel.

From the Mouth of the Case Study

Another storytelling approach is to have the person in the case study (or vignette) speak for him or herself. They can speak directly to the reader about their experiences in their own words. It can be compelling to read an account directly from the source.

Cliffhangers

You know the cliffhanger. Think of watching TV and you hear a shot ring out; you know someone is injured, but you don't know who it is or how badly they have been hurt. The storytellers promise that if you tune in next week, you might just find out the answer.

You can use this technique with your vignettes. Give your reader the setup, but don't reveal the ending. Let them know that you will return to this story later in the book. By doing this, you are giving your reader another reason to want to turn those pages.

FAQs on Storytelling

Q: Do the Vignettes Need to Be True?

A: My rule of thumb here is to be honest with your audience. If the story is true but you are changing the name or some identifying markers, then let your reader know. If you are writing about a typical client, but not a specific client, let the reader know. If you are combining several of your most interesting cases, let the reader know. In my case for this book, though the stories are based on real people and events, identifying factors such as names, descriptors, or book topics have been changed either to protect the identity or the concept of their book.

Q: How Do I Choose the Stories? I Have so Many.

A: Create your "typical client" avatar. Who are they? What do they struggle with? Come up with the top five to ten most common issues that people bring to you. Make sure you have a vignette that represents the most common issues that you see walk into your office. The reason to have a variety of vignettes is that people want to find themselves (and what they struggle with) in the book.

Q: Should I Be Funny?

A: Be yourself. If you are a funny person, then your stories may
be funny and entertaining naturally, but don't feel that you
need to turn into a comedian. Be authentic. That is what the
reader is seeking most—an authentic connection with you,
their guide.

Should I Tell MY Story?

> *Owning our story can be hard but not nearly as difficult
> as spending our lives running from it. Embracing our
> vulnerabilities is risky but not nearly as dangerous as giving
> up on love and belonging and joy—the experiences that
> make us the most vulnerable.*
>
> —Brené Brown, *The Gifts of Imperfection*

Many authors wonder if they should include their own story in
their book. My short answer is "Yes, and…."

First, the "yes."

Yes, you should allow your readers to know you and how you
came to your beliefs, thoughts, and opinions. Your reader wants
to feel a sense of closeness. Plus, it is incredibly empowering to
own your story by sharing it. (Trust me, I'm a memoir teacher.)

Next, the "and…."

The "and" is that you must decide on the tone of your book. Here
are some guidelines

- Make sure the focus of your book is on your reader.
- If you want the focus of your book to be your story, then
  it's possible you may want to write a memoir. (Nothing
  wrong with that, ladies—see below.)

- Carefully place your stories so they directly support your ideas.
- Watch out for oversharing.

Q: So, What Is the Right Amount of Sharing Vs. TMI (Too Much Information)?

A: I'm repeating myself, but it's a crucial point: you want to keep the focus on your reader. It's about them, not you. Share enough so they can know you and understand you, but if it ever feels like you are writing more about you than them, time to tone it down or switch to memoir. A good editor can help you with this issue, as sometimes it's hard to tell if you have ventured into the TMI zone.

Approach Question #3: How would you describe your writer's voice?

Your writer's voice is how the reader will describe the tone of the book. Will they say it was funny, light, and easy to read? Will they say it was insightful and meticulously researched? Will they say it was informative and empowering? Everyone has a writer's voice, they just may not know what it is, or trust themselves enough to use it.

Your writing **VOICE** should reflect you.

- Your writing voice is often what makes the approach fresh or unique. In other words, the information may be "out there," but you are presenting it in a humorous or tell-it-like-it-is manner that makes the approach new.
- Often, the voice will be revealed in the title. (Think: *Eat Mangoes Naked: Finding Pleasure Everywhere and Dancing with the Pits* by Sark or *No Excuses: Nine Ways Women Can Change How We Think about Power* by Gloria Feldt.)

IF YOU THINK YOU WANT TO WRITE A MEMOIR

I teach memoir writing and love the art form. Memoirs can absolutely be thought leading books, though most follow a narrative template. This means that they focus on the story itself and read like a novel.

If you are venturing down this path, let me offer a few tidbits. Memoirs are on the cutting edge of innovation, often breaking rules and inventing new ones. Having said that, I often break memoirs into two categories:

1. Tell Me a Story → A full narrative with a beginning, middle, and end. This is the bulk of most memoirs, and they almost read like a (fictional) novel.

    Examples of Tell Me a Story: *Wild: From Lost to Found on the Pacific Crest Trail* by Cheryl Strayed or *The Glass Castle: A Memoir* by Jeannette Walls

2. Beads on a String → A series of short stories connected by a theme.

    Examples of Beads on a String: *Gift From the Sea* by Anne Morrow Lindbergh or *We're Going to Need More Wine: Stories* by Gabrielle Union

Note: If you want to write a narrative memoir, the templates presented below will not work. You will want to grab my first book, *7 Essential Writing Tools*, which will guide you through the basics of narrative writing.

Q: Can a Memoir Be a Thought Leader Book?

A: Absolutely. In fact, I opened this book with a discussion of Maya Angelou's groundbreaking memoir, *I Know Why the Caged Bird Sings*. Let's take a look at five more examples of memoirs that continue to influence our culture, our conversations, and our lives.

1. *Reading Lolita in Tehran: A Memoir in Books* by Azar Nafisi. Her story as a teacher in Iran who secretly encouraged a small group of students to read western classics furthered the discussion on women's

education in the Middle East, restrictive dress codes, speaking one's mind, and limits on personal freedom.

2. *I Feel Bad About My Neck: And Other Thoughts on Being a Woman* by Nora Ephron who crafted this funny, insightful, and poignant collection of essays on what it means to age as a woman in modern American society. With her signature dry wit, she tackles empty nests, menopause, and the ups and downs of maintaining an aging woman's body.

3. *The Glass Castle: A Memoir* by Jeannette Walls is an unflinching, powerful discussion of poverty and homelessness, and a brave discussion of a dysfunctional parenting experience filled with both tremendous neglect and tremendous love.

4. *Girl, Interrupted* by Susanna Kaysen is a portrait of a young woman who attempted suicide, was diagnosed with borderline personality disorder, and spent almost two years in a psychiatric hospital in the 1960s. Kaysen's book questions the definitions of sane and insane, and helped to open up a discussion about mental illness and psychiatric hospitals.

5. *Love Warrior: A Memoir* by Glennon Doyle Melton. This book is a rich discussion of infidelity, fierce self-discovery, and one's relationship to the divine. Faced with the possible ending of her marriage, Melton takes the reader through an exploration of letting go of societal messages and diving deep into one's most vulnerable self to find what is most authentic.

Q: How is a Beads on a String Memoir Different From the Stories Template?

A: In a Beads on a String memoir, the focus will be on you, the writer, and your memoir experiences. Usually, all the stories are about the author. In the Stories Template, the focus will be on your reader and how the stories can help the reader in some specific way. Often the stories are from a variety of authors.

Writer's Voice: Examples From the Bookshelf

EXAMPLE 1

You Are a Badass:
How to Stop Doubting Your Greatness
and Start Living an Awesome Life
by Jen Sincero

Sincero's voice is entertaining, feisty, and inspiring. She encourages the reader to challenge their self-sabotaging beliefs and behaviors using humorous stories, swear words, and direct advice. Her style is approachable and bold.

EXAMPLE 2

Presence: Bringing Your Boldest Self to Your Biggest Challenges
by Amy Cuddy

Cuddy's voice is charming, humble, and informative. She draws from extensive behavioral science research and combines it with authenticity and inspiration. Her style is intelligent and openhearted.

EXAMPLE 3

Help, Thanks, Wow: The Three Essential Prayers
by Anne Lamott

Lamott's voice is authentic, brutally honest, and deeply insightful. She breaks down the complex world that prayer can be into simple and sage instruction. She shares her deepest thoughts, struggles, and worries as if the reader were a best friend. Her style is authentic, intimate, and thought provoking.

Note: There is no right or wrong way to have a voice or a tone. What is important is that you know what your voice is, and that you boldly claim it as your own.

Finding Your Voice

We want YOU! That's right, YOU! The way you share the material should stem from who you are authentically. There are many ways to express one's writing voice. Look over the following words and see if any of these descriptive words resonate with you.

Intellectual	Raw
Contemplative	Fierce
Lyrical	Nurturing
Funny	Wild
Satirical	Spiritual
Confrontational	Analytical
Direct	Simple
To the point	Bold
Passionate	Calming

If You Are Not Sure About Your Writing Voice, Answer These Questions

1. How would you describe your speaking voice?
2. How might those close to you describe your speaking voice?
3. Do you tend to be direct and to the point or do you deliver information in a softer, gentler manner?
4. Do you make people laugh?
5. Do you make people think deeply?
6. Do you often reference research or statistics when making an argument?
7. Do you use personal stories to illustrate a point?
8. Do you share parts of your own life with others?
9. Do people tend to describe you as more quiet or loud?

Karen and Ruby

Karen was a depressed, thirty-two-year-old mother of two. She had never experienced depression before and was confused about the causes of her sadness. She was in a job that she loved but found herself locked away in an office cubicle for nine to ten hours a day. She loved being outside in nature daily and had spent most of her twenties as a surf instructor. Once she had her children, she found she couldn't afford to live on her surf instructor's salary. She moved to a desk job for a company that sold surfing materials. Karen didn't quite understand what was going on inside of her. She only knew that she found herself feeling lower and lower, to the point that she dreaded going in to work.

Ruby was a city-based therapist and a nature specialist. For years she had conducted her sessions in her office, until there was a flood in her building that caused her to have a few of her sessions outside in nature. Ruby was surprised to find that her outdoor sessions provided stronger results than those within the office walls. Ruby began conducting her sessions outside, even creating an outdoor office in a garden setting. Clients shared with Ruby that that they loved the chance to be in nature. Ruby dove into the research surrounding nature deficit disorder, which showed that reconnecting with nature can improve energy and mood and can boost an overall sense of well-being. Ruby expanded her practice to include gardening therapy sessions. Clients worked in a garden while processing their issues. She created week-long retreats in a lakeside center with a flourishing garden. It wasn't clinical research, but Ruby observed that the clients with depression who created a regular connection with nature experienced an almost-fifty-percent mood improvement. Ruby decided to write a book about how anyone can create a simple nature routine to improve their overall sense of well-being.

Karen, who had once thrived and never experienced depression, had lost her connection to the natural world.

What did Karen need?

Ruby's book.

How Ruby Answered the Approach Questions

Who is the star of my show: Big Ideas, Stories, or a Plan-of-Action?

Ruby saw breakthroughs with her city-dwelling clients by allowing them to experience nature while in session. Her big idea was, no matter how tech-connected and city-loving a person tends to be, creating a regular nature connection routine can improve mood and enhance a sense of well-being. She offered a shift in thinking and was drawn to the Big Ideas Template.

How is this book fresh or unique?

Ruby felt that the wisdom she was imparting was ancient. Yet, she explained, as she looked around the world today, she saw that our society was no longer in touch with that wisdom. What Ruby offered was a way to take ancient wisdom and bring it to a modern, city-based clientele.

How would you describe your writer's voice?

Ruby's speaking voice was soothing, lighthearted, and gentle. She wanted her book to reflect her calm demeanor and meditative tone.

Key #3: Approach Worksheet

Who is the star of your show?

(Place an "X" on your chosen template.)

Big Ideas   __

Stories   __

Plan-of-Action   __

How is your book fresh or unique? _____

_____

_____

How would you describe your writer's voice? _____

_____

_____

_____

_____

Bite-Sized Thoughts for Chapter 8

1. Key #3, or the Approach, involves the *how* of your book. How can you organize and present your ideas in the most dynamic way possible?

2. The first Approach Question is: *Who is the star of my show? Big Ideas, Stories, or a Plan-of- Action?*

3. The second Approach Question is: *How is my book fresh or unique?* Finding a fresh approach means that you have a fun or new way of presenting the information, or that you are adding to the discussion in a way that shows you are one step ahead of the curve. One surefire way to engage your audience, and almost guarantee freshness, is to learn how to tell a good story. Stories evoke emotions, illustrate facts, and create a bond between writer and reader.

4. The third Approach Question is: *How would you describe your writer's voice?* Your writing **voice** is the style in which you communicate to your reader. Your voice should reflect the real you. Often, the writer's voice will be revealed in the title.

5. To provide you with organizational maps of how to present your ideas, there are three Dynamic Thought Leader Templates you can choose from

   - Big Ideas
   - Stories
   - Plan-of-Action

CHAPTER 9

A LITTLE STYLE
GOES A LONG WAY

From the Back of the Mountain Hut to the Edge of the Red Sea

In my wacky twenties, I spent some time in a Bedouin village in Dahab, Egypt. I stayed with a few friends in a glamorous hut-like situation at the base of a rocky mountainside. The hut boasted nothing except that it was ridiculously cheap, and it was only a ten-minute walk, to the beautiful Red Sea. The problem with that ten-minute walk was that you had to make your way around seriously huge boulders, while you avoided tripping over rocks or falling into snake holes. (I don't know if they were snake holes, but something lived down there, something I did not want to meet.)

Early one morning, I made my way out the back, and yes, true to advertising, within a ten-minute walk I was at the gorgeous sea. Unfortunately, by the time I had jumped over the boulders and fell into about five of the snake holes, I had twisted my ankle so bad, my friends had to carry me back from the sea. I cursed that rocky, unstable path.

The next time I made my way out to the sea, I only fell down four times.

The next time I made my way out the sea after that, I fell down two times.

After a few weeks, I was able to make my way from the hut to sea without falling, twisting my ankle, or cursing anything. Why? I had learned to avoid the holes and navigate the path. I knew where the widest snake hole was just by the big brown boulder. I knew where the deepest snake hole was just by a patch of spiky rocks. Eventually, I even found a shortcut that allowed me to avoid jumping from the biggest boulder onto the shore.

Learning to Write Is a Lifelong Adventure

If you continue on this path (and I hope you do), you will find that you will grow as a writer for the rest of your life. Every time you set pen to paper or write a new draft, you will be adopting new skill sets and polishing your craft.

There are some common pitfalls in writing a thought leader book. Different writers tend to trip over the same snake holes and fall off the same large boulders. Below you will find seventeen of my tips and tools to avoid the most common writing pitfalls. Consider me your guide from the back of the mountain hut to the edge of the Red Sea.

17 Tips to Avoid the Snake Holes and Boulders (Or My Top Nonfiction Writing Tips)

Note: Many of these tips involve style choices. (Meaning if it works for you, captures your style, and expresses what you want to say, go for it.)

1. Own Your Knowledge

The world needs your ideas. It's time to start sharing them fully, loudly, boldly, slowly—without diminishment or apology.

—Tara Mohr

When it comes to our communication styles, women have some good things and some not-so-good things going for us. On the positive side, women tend to be collaborative and inclusive. We want to share our information and empower others. On the not-so-positive side, women tend to apologize, justify, backpedal, second guess, and soften their expertise.

What if there was a way to both empower others and own our expertise? What if you could be inclusive and step into your authority all at once?

Here Are Some Quick and Dirty "Owning It" Tips

- Remove unnecessary modifiers. When you use modifiers, you are communicating that you need to qualify why you have a point in the first place. No need to do that. Make your point. Examples: "really," "pretty," "virtually," "rather," "very," "kind of," "actually," "basically," "practically."
- Remove "just," "I just want to say," "If I could just add," "There is just one more thing."
- Remove "I think," "I suggest," "I wonder if we should," "In my opinion," "I believe."
- Use affirming, declarative language. "I recommend," "The research shows that," "We know."
- Don't substitute a question for a statement.
- Avoid undermining your own points by using phrases such as, "You may disagree but," "I'm not an expert but I see it this way," "Other research may show differing conclusions but…."

2. Use an Active Voice Over a Passive Voice

When you use a passive voice, it means that the reader must work harder to understand your meaning. When the voice is active, the meaning is clear. The subject is doing the action.

> Active Voice = subject acts upon an object
> Passive Voice = object is acted upon by subject

Passive: Sarah was known by me.
Active: I know Sarah.

Passive: The couple was helped by the communication tool.
Active: The communication tool helped the couple.

Passive: Research will be presented by the association.
Active: The association will present their research.

3. Avoid Clichés—Because All That Glitters Is Most Definitely Not Gold

A cliché is an overused expression. It has been used so much, that we may not notice that we are using one, and a reader may not even notice or understand the meaning of the writing.

Examples

- Every cloud has a silver lining
- As long as we are all on the same page at the end of the day
- Think outside the box
- Read between the lines
- Time heals all wounds
- Laughter is the best medicine
- When life gives you lemons, make lemonade
- In the current climate
- All for one, and one for all
- All's well that ends well
- Haste makes waste
- What goes around, comes around

4. IBC Your Paragraphs

Your book is made up of paragraphs. They are the bricks in your building. A handy dandy paragraph-building guideline to follow is the IBC rule → introduction, body, conclusion.

Introduction

- Step One: Know your topic (pick one topic per paragraph).
- Step Two: Use a strong topic sentence that communicates the main idea of the paragraph.
- Step One: Know your topic (pick one topic per paragraph).
- Step Two: Use a strong topic sentence that communicates the main idea of the paragraph.

Body

- Step Three: Illuminate your point with supportive details. The body usually includes three to five sentences where you offer examples, evidence, or an application of the idea. Make these sentences clear and simple.

Conclusion

- Step Four: Craft a concluding sentence; one that sums up your ideas and links back to your topic sentence.

5. Short Sentences Are Delicious Sentences

> *There's not much to be said about the period except that most writers don't reach it soon enough.*
>
> —William Zinsser

The general rule is that sentences should be around twenty words long. It's also a general rule that you should vary the lengths of your sentences for variety. When you can, shorten your sentences without sacrificing your message. Readers know when filler is filler. So, if you can cut out a word or two, do it. If you can cut a phrase, do it. Readers appreciate a writer who is concise.

Common unnecessary phrases: "Due to the fact that," "in the event that," "first and foremost," "as a matter of fact," "as far as I'm concerned," "chances are that."

Common unnecessary words (also known as intensifiers): extremely, very, severely, really.

To sum it up: Know your idea, write a draft, cut the fluff, and trust that your reader will get the message.

6. Begin Strong, End Strong

Begin

Can you capture your meaning right up front? Start your sentences or paragraphs off strong by using subjects and verbs. State your meaning early.

Example of a weak beginning: If you look at the statistics, more and more women are entering the medical field.

Fix: Women are entering the medical field in record numbers.

End

Can you end on a crisp declaration or a satisfying point? Try to end your sentences by pulling your point into clear focus. Think of the way a gymnast nails a landing. That's how you want the end of your sentences to feel; you want them to have a strong finish.

Avoid Ending Sentences With These Words

- From
- On

- In
- At
- To
- With

Example of a weak ending: Speaking is one skill set that women on the collegiate debate team are naturally gifted at.

Fix: Women on the collegiate debate team are naturally gifted at speaking.

7. No Need to Out-Fancy Your Reader

> *Do not be tempted by a twenty-dollar word when there is a ten-center handy, ready and able.*
>
> —Strunk and White

Sometimes we feel the need to get fancy and use big words. Pull yourself back from that impulse. Your job as a thought leader is to take complex information and make it easy to understand. Using obscure or hard to pronounce words may only serve to confuse or alienate your reader. Do you know that the front page of the *Wall Street Journal* is written for an eighth-grade level? True story.

8. NO NEED TO SHOUT!!

One way in which we, writers, mistrust our readers is to assume they will not understand our message. For example, we, writers, often <u>unnecessarily underline</u>, use ALL CAPS, or use exclamation points!! Too much emphasis can cheapen your message, connote overexcitement or an emergency, or call attention when it isn't needed. Bottom line: To be effective, use these emphasis techniques sparingly.

9. Avoid Redundancy Because You Don't Need to Say It Again and Again

Here is another way that we, writers, mistrust our readers. We fear that our reader will not understand our intended message, so we say the same thing twice.

Watch out for pleonasm, which is a term that describes a phrase that is, in and of itself, redundant.

Examples: "I finally fell asleep at twelve midnight," or "I wrote an autobiography about my life," or "I saw the biggest tree in the forest with my own eyes." "The vote was totally unanimous" or "her guidelines were absolutely essential."

Watch out for using two words or two phrases that mean the same thing when one will do the job.

Examples: The teacher was articulate and well spoken. The discussion was fruitful and yielded results. The work was sloppy and messy.

Quick Fix: Pick the strongest words or phrases that say what you want to say and cut the rest.

10. Adverbs Are Not Your Friends (but they are not your enemies either)

The road to hell is paved with adverbs.

—Stephen King

Adverbs generally come in the form of an "ly" word. Think: nervously, slowly, loudly. Writers gravitate toward the use of adverbs to enhance meaning, to add a splash of color, or to accurately portray how people speak. And yet, many writers and editors consider adverbs to be the sign of either a lazy writer or an overwritten piece. The reason is because adverbs can clutter up a good sentence. When I was a young writer I was told, "Unless the adverb changes the meaning of the verb, cut it." However, I still like my precisely placed adverbs.

The "LY" Check: After you have completed your first draft, check your manuscript for "ly" words. Ask yourself, is there a stronger verb I can use? If not, it's okay to keep a few here and there.

11. Curb the Run-On Sentences

A run-on sentence occurs when two or more complete sentences (or independent clauses) are connected improperly.

Sample sentence: Meditation can decrease your stress plus if you meditate daily it can also improve your concentration.

Fixes

- Split the sentence into two smaller sentences by using a period. (Works well when the sentences are long. Just don't overdo it with too many short, choppy sentences.)
  - Meditation can decrease your stress levels. If you meditate daily, you may find your concentration improved.

- Use a comma and a coordinating conjunction (like *or, and, but*)
  - Meditation can decrease your stress, and if you meditate daily, it can also improve concentration.

- Use a semicolon. When you put a semicolon between two independent clauses the sentence is grammatically correct.
  - Meditation can decrease your stress; meditating daily can improve concentration.

12. Make the Text Eye-Pleasing

While this is often a stylistic choice, I encourage you to make your text pleasing to the modern reader's eye. That means making it scannable. One quick and dirty scannable trick is to use clear subheadings.

The following stylistic tools can make your text more inviting; just don't overdo it.

- Bulleted lists
- Numbered lists
- Use of white space
- Highlighting, bolding, italicizing
- Takeaways

13. Pick Your Reference-Books Buddies

Every writer has a few books that they will return to over and over for reference. These are some of my favorites:

- *Bird by Bird: Some Instructions on Writing and Life* by Anne Lamott (Funny, wise advice on writing and the writing world)
- *On Writing: A Memoir of the Craft* by Stephen King (King shares inspiring advice, helpful tips, and personal experiences about his life as a writer)
- *The Chicago Manual of Style* by The University of Chicago Press Editorial Staff (Often considered the definitive guide for clear and accurate communication)
- *The Elements of Style* by William Strunk Jr. and E.B. White (What many consider to be the classic English style guide; there have been many revisions and editions by a variety of authors)
- *On Writing Well: The Classic Guide to Writing Nonfiction* by William Zinsser (For three generations it has been a well-

respected nonfiction writing guide for editors, writers, and journalists)
- *The Artist's Way: A Spiritual Path to Higher Creativity* by Julia Cameron (Cameron guides the reader on a twelve-week journey to uncover their creative process and to spark inner joy for being an artist)
- Note: There are some websites I have also become addicted to such as GrammarGirl, Grammarly, the online dictionary Merriam-Webster, and Thesaurus.com).

14. Flow, Flow, Flow

Each paragraph should be related to the main idea of the chapter. Each paragraph should develop logically from the one before. That is the essence of flow. But don't fret about flow when you are in the dreaming or first-draft phase. Flow often happens as you rewrite (so be patient with yourself).

15. Use Succinct, Fresh Images (Get Inspired by Haiku)

When you want to paint a picture for your reader, the best images are the ones that are crisp and original. Use your unique experiences to describe, add color, or evoke emotion. Studying the art of haiku (a Japanese poetic form with usually only 17 syllables) can help new writers learn how to create a vivid image with few words.

Consider this translation of a haiku by Japanese wandering poet Matsuo Basho, written in 1687:

> old pond:
> frog leaps in
> the sound of water

In just a few words, Basho manages to create a succinct and vivid image. It takes practice, but your writing will benefit from learning this art form (not to mention what it will do to heighten your Twitter abilities).

Two Books I Like on Haiku: *Haiku Mind: 108 Poems to Cultivate Awareness and Open Your Heart* by Patricia Donegan and *The Heart of Haiku* by Jane Hirshfield

16. Your Voice Is the Magic Dust (so be you and only you)

Readers want to follow a guide that is genuine. Readers want to trust a narrator that is real. And that, my friend, is you. Don't shy away from your own unique patterns of speech, even if you break the rules. Be authoritative, but be yourself.

17. Make All the Mistakes in This Chapter, Then Trust the Editing Process

First drafters, stay dreamy. Yes, these are all important guidelines—but don't overthink them while you are in the "pour it all out" stage. For creativity to flow, you may need to forget these rules for a while. Rules can clog up your creative process. Trust that when you are done writing, you will take a nice healthy break. Then, when you are ready, you will come back and read your manuscript with fresh eyes. I suggest that you read it out loud, so you can hear the sound of your words. Listen to the rhythm and the way that they flow. Then make changes to your heart's content. And don't forget that you can and will hire or work with an editor or editors. Said editors will be checking for content, flow, grammar, and all that jazz. Make mistakes. A ton of mistakes. The career of editing would not exist if writers were perfect.

Bite-Sized Thoughts for Chapter 9

1. Women tend to be collaborative and inclusive communicators. We also tend to apologize, justify, and soften our expertise. Remove language that justifies, qualifies, or undermines your authority. Own your expertise.

2. Common mistakes that writers make are run-on sentences, repetitive language, passive sentences, weak beginnings and endings of sentences, use of clichés, and overuse of adverbs, caps, underlining, and exclamation points.

3. Learn how to sculpt paragraphs using the four steps of the IBC method:

    Introduction

    Step One: Know your topic (pick one topic per paragraph).

    Step Two: Use a strong topic sentence that communicates the main idea of the paragraph.

    Body

    Step Three: Illuminate your point with supportive details. The body usually includes three to five sentences where you offer examples, evidence or an application of the idea. Make these sentences clear and simple.

    Conclusion

    Step Four: Craft a concluding sentence; one that sums up your ideas and links back to your topic sentence.

4. Studying the art of the haiku, a poem with 17 syllables, can help writers learn how to craft succinct and vivid images.

5. Trust the editing process. There is a reason all writers travel through stages of writing and editing. Meaning, there is

a time to be free flowing so that you can get your ideas on paper. Allow yourself to make lots and lots of mistakes during the free-flowing first draft. Know that the time will come to put on your editor's hat and trim, sculpt, and shape to your heart's content.

Now it's time to take a closer look at the Dynamic Thought Leader Templates and decide which one fits you and the style of book you are writing.

PART THREE

MAKE IT YOUR OWN

CHAPTER 10

THE DYNAMIC THOUGHT LEADER BOOK TEMPLATES

The Crunchy Stuff

One day when my son was seven-years-old, we sat under a big oak tree and looked up at the clumps of leaves and branches. We talked about what shapes the leaves and branches made. He said that one looked like a dragon on a super-fast skateboard. I said that one looked like a bird with three eyes and a super-long nose.

I leaned in and asked him, "If you were going to write a story, right now, would you rather write about a dragon on a skateboard or a bird with three eyes and a super-long nose?"

He smiled and said, "I like this, Mama, I like talking with you about the dreamy stuff."

"What do you mean?" I asked.

"Well, ya know, there is dreamy stuff and crunchy stuff. We talk about lots of kinds of things. But I like the dreamy stuff better."

"Huh, I didn't know that. So, what is the crunchy stuff?"

"You know, Mama, that's like when you tell me how to do stuff. Like, this much peanut butter goes here, and then this much jelly goes here, or adding up the pennies to make sure they are a dime. Crunchy stuff."

I giggled. Knowing there was a place for both: for dreaming, and for the well-made peanut butter and jelly sandwich. (Crust to crust is a must.)

So, that's where we find ourselves now. We have done a lot of brainstorming, dreaming, and scheming; and, now, it is time to get crunching.

 ZOOMING OUT: How to Decide on Your Template
To help you think through the decision regarding which structure might be right for you, we are going to zoom out and look at three ways you can organize your book.

Quick Reminder #1

These Are the Templates

Big Ideas
Stories
Plan-of-Action

Quick Reminder #2

Your book may contain all three (Big Ideas, Stories, and a Plan-of-Action), but ask yourself, *which one is the star of the show?* Which one is the focus of the book, where you will spend most of your time? Are the ideas the star of the show? Are the stories the star of the show? Or, is the plan-of-action the star of the show? When you can answer that, you will know which template to choose.

Know that each template can be individualized, depending upon your approach. So, don't think of the templates as a strict outline, but as more of a general guide.

The book you are holding in your hands is primarily a Big Ideas book, but there is a heavy emphasis on plan-of-action. I call it a Big Ideas book because my call to action, (*Please ladies, we need you, get out there and write your book now!),* is the star of the show. But the templates, worksheets, and tools (the Plan-of-Action parts) are my backup dancers. The book reflects who I am and how I work. I love big ideas but need tools to help me to make those big ideas a reality. Also, don't knock backup dancers. They offer value, razzle-dazzle, and can kick really high.

A Note About Chapters 11, 12, and 13

After each template is presented, I will walk you through a series of examples from the bookshelf. These books have made it to a bestseller list, won an award, made an impact on our culture, or lasted the test of time. The titles span decades, and I have attempted to cover a broad subject matter. I am not promoting these books in and of themselves (though I like 'em!). I just want to illustrate how notable female authors have structured their books. I tend to learn by example, so looking over successful books (that speak to you) might be what teaches and inspires you as well.

E-book Note: If you are thinking about writing an e-book only, you can modify any of the templates. Remember that the super-short e-book runs about 3,000–5,000 words. The short e-book runs about 10,000–15,000 words and the average-length e-book runs about 25,000 words.

ZOOMING IN: What's in a Chapter?
At the end of each template, we are going to zoom in and discuss the chapter recipes. While the template is the outline for your entire book, your chapter recipe is the outline for the individual chapters. Know that there is no one right or perfect recipe. The only recipe is the one that you think best supports the ideas in your book. You do not need to adhere to the same recipe for each chapter; you can mix it up with what I have come to call Anchors and Variables.

Chapter Anchors and Variables

 Anchors: You will see these in every chapter, such as a quote that starts each chapter or cartoon that ends each chapter.

 Variables: These are segments that vary from chapter to chapter.

For example, you may want to start every chapter with a relevant statistic. The statistics would be an anchor.

You may want to have supportive vignettes in most, but not all the chapters. In this case, the vignettes would be a variable.

Q: So, What Exactly Is a Chapter Recipe?

A: It's all the ingredients that can go into each chapter. Often each chapter will have the same formula (but this is not necessary).

Possible Ingredients for Your Chapter Recipe

Quotes	Journaling questions
Vignettes	Worksheets
Infographics	Stories
Charts	Cartoons
Poems	Exercises
Song lyrics	Drawings
Sample scripts	Practices
Prayers	Did You Know?
Top 5 Ways to …	Bulleted lists
(or Top 3 or Top 7)	Fun text boxes
Questions	Reminders
Allegories	Self-analysis quizzes
Affirmations	Personal stories
Statistics	Research
Myths	Takeaways

Chapters Have Personalities

Just as your book has its own personality, so do the chapters. Usually, the personality of the book and the personality of the chapters reflect and enhance one another. For example, Martha Beck's *The Joy Diet: 10 Daily Practices for a Happier Life* is a book that has an upbeat-yet-wise personality, evident by its title. The chapters reflect Beck's smart and playful style with humorously provocative chapter titles and bite-sized bits of practical wisdom.

Questions to Help You Build Your Chapter

- What do you want the reader to feel as they read your book?
  - Bold
  - Joyous
  - A sense of fun
  - Contemplative
  - Inspired

- o Meditative
- o Empowered
- o Captivated
- o Supported
- o Intelligent
- o Strong
- o Informed
- o Whimsical
- o Fill in your own word

- How interactive do you want your chapters to be?

- Do you have any personal stories that might help illuminate the discussion?

- Would graphics or infographics help support your ideas?

- Would research or case studies help support your ideas?

- Would quotes or excerpts help support your ideas?

- Do you want your reader to reflect on any big ideas through journaling or meditations?

- Do you want your reader to process any big ideas through tools or exercises?

One Way to Construct a Chapter → Present Information Like Aristotle

Tell 'em what you're going to tell 'em. Tell 'em. Tell 'em what you told 'em.

You may have heard this advice if you were trained in the art of giving a speech. First, you tell your audience what you are going to present, then you present it, and then you recap what you just presented. This advice has been attributed to many thinkers, from Aristotle to Dale Carnegie. This method of clarity and repetition will help people to remember and better understand your information.

How "Tell 'Em" Works

1.   **Tell them what you will tell them.** (Often, in the first paragraph.) Here you will explain why you are covering this topic, how it will be of help to the reader, or support your larger argument. Tell your reader what the info is, and why it is important for them to read it. This section does not have to be long.

2.   **Tell them.** Here you can be as creative as you want to be. Share the information using your voice. Give your reader the content and support it with details, research, or stories. Or infographics, drawings, or musings. However, you want to express your most salient arguments; remember to always keep your reader in mind. They are turning pages, wondering how this information will be of service to them.

3.   **Tell them what you just told them.** (Usually the closing paragraph.) Here, you will reiterate the major ideas you have presented to your reader. Often, in a book, this is done with takeaways (as you see in this book) or final thoughts. When you write this section, ask yourself: *If my reader only remembered a few points of knowledge from this chapter, what should they be?*

Q: If I Follow This Formula, Won't My Chapters Be Boring and Predictable?

A: Not at all. Because you have structure, it doesn't mean that the text can't have its own style and personality. Your words should still be fun, original, and fresh. Remember that you, being you, is the magic.

Q: Do I Have to Use the "Tell 'Em" Formula?

A: How you present your information is entirely up to you. I like this formula because it offers a beginning, middle, and end shape to your concepts. It introduces your intentions, creates a space to offer your main ideas, and then provides gentle repetition. This simple recipe has helped information to stick inside the noggins of my students.

Bite-Sized Thoughts for Chapter 10

1. In this chapter, we discussed three Dynamic Thought
    Leader Templates to help you create a basic structure for
    your book.

    The Big Ideas Template is → the most common and
    universal template. This template illuminates a core
    concept. It asks the reader to make a shift in their thinking
    or offers a call to action.

    The Stories Template is → filled with one big story or lots
    of little stories, vignettes, or reflections that illuminate the
    theme of the book.

    The Plan-of-Action Template is → highly actionable and
    offers clear advice for success. This template is the most
    directive, and it involves following a concrete plan, or a
    series of steps, toward a specific end-goal.

    Your book may contain all three—big ideas, stories, and a
    plan-of-action—but what the templates ask you to decide
    is, *which one is the star of the show?*

2. Each chapter will contain anchors and variables. Anchors
    are repeating segments that you will see reliably, in every
    chapter. Variables are the elements that vary from one
    chapter to the next.

3. Every chapter has a recipe. Some writers utilize the same
    chapter recipe, and others mix it up. Some ingredients
    you may want to sprinkle throughout your chapters are
    quotes, infographics, vignettes, lists, journaling questions,
    self-analysis quizzes, affirmations, statistics, worksheets,
    cartoons, and takeaways. **Don't overdo it.** Use only what is
    illuminating, necessary, and helpful.

4. Chapters have personalities. Asking questions such as, *what do I want my reader to feel?* and, *how interactive do I want my chapters to be?* can help you to brainstorm the personality of your chapters.

5. The "Tell 'Em" formula is helpful for creating an easy and understandable chapter flow. First, you tell your reader what ideas you are going to present, then present your ideas with examples and supportive information, and finally, recap the ideas you just presented.

CHAPTER 11

THE BIG IDEAS TEMPLATE

The Big Ideas Template is the most common and universal. It encompasses a big core concept or a larger call to action that may require a shift in consciousness.

With this template, the information is usually broken up into parts (or sections) with chapters underneath those parts. Usually, chapter one (or two) covers the overall theory, and the last chapter offers a summary, conclusion, and a call to action.

If you are planning to use this template, your book will focus on some big call to action, like think big, awaken your inner genius, view your personality or temperament in a different way, believe in your power to lead, learn how to create wealth, create a life where you can thrive, trust the flow of the universe, reframe how you see failure, understand your mind, or invigorate your soul.

The Parts of the Big Ideas Template

Front Matter (The Setup)

- Praise for
- Dedication
- Table of contents

- Introduction
  - Defining the problem → the bad news
  - Defining my idea → the good news (or, why read the book)
  - Why I wrote this book; a bit about me
  - A call to turn the page
- Other options for front matter
  - A quote or a phrase
  - Author's note
  - Foreword

Body Matter (Core Content of the Book)

- Parts/Sections/Chapters—in that order
  - Part One
    - Chapter 1: Overview of the book (reason why this book is an answer to your problem)
    - Chapters 2-3
  - Part Two
    - Chapters 3-6
  - Part Three
    - Chapters 7-10
  - Close → (Often a hope, wish, or call to action)
    - One or two chapters that summarize the material and offer a specific call to action or a call to join a community

End Matter (Optional Wrap-up Materials at the Back of the Book)

- Afterword
- About the author
- Index
- Notes
- Chapter from next book

- Other optional end matter
  - Glossary
  - Appendix
  - Bibliography
  - Reader's guide
  - Recommended reading
  - Resources
  - Tips for parents (or educators)
  - Interview with the author

The Big Ideas Template: Examples From the Bookshelf

To gain a better understanding, let's go to the bookshelf and look at some books that follow the Big Ideas Template.

Remember: These books are in the Big Ideas Template because the ideas, call to action, or call for a shift in consciousness are the stars of the show. The book may still contain stories and plans of action, but they are the backup players.

EXAMPLE 1

Quiet: The Power of Introverts in a World
That Can't Stop Talking
by Susan Cain

Front Matter (The Setup)

- "A Manifesto for Introverts"
- A (seriously) brief dedication
- A quote from Allan Shawn
- Table of contents
- Author's note
- Introduction

- o Defining the problem → the bad news. The US is an extroverted nation that often endorses the extroverted personality as the ideal personality type.
- o Defining your idea → the good news (or, why read the book). Introverts are, and have always been, powerful. Extroverts should not underestimate the talents or gifts of introverts. Being quiet and cerebral is a cause for celebration, and, throughout the book, Cain will tell you why.
- o An informal quiz to see if you are an introvert
- o A call to action: Cain hopes the book offers permission and an excitement just to be yourself in the world.

Body Matter (Core Content of the Book)

- Part One: The Extrovert Ideal
  - o Part One contains three chapters that cover topics such as how the extrovert is seen as the cultural ideal, how personality works in leadership, and exploring the pros and cons of working within a group or working alone.

- Part Two: Your Biology, Your Self?
  - o Part Two contains four chapters that cover topics such as temperament, nature and nurture, free will, public speaking for introverts, and the differences in how introverts and extroverts think and process dopamine.

- Part Three: Do All Cultures Have an Extrovert Ideal?
  - o Part Three contains only one chapter and discusses Asian Americans and the concept of soft power.

- Part Four: How to Love, How to Work
  - o Part Four contains four chapters and covers topics like deciding when you should act more extroverted,

how to communicate with extroverts, and raising an introverted child. Part Four ends with a conclusion.

End Matter (Optional Wrap-up Materials at the Back of the Book)

- A Note on the dedication
- A Note on the words "introvert" and "extrovert"
- Acknowledgments
- Notes
- Index
- *Quiet*: A Reader's Guide: The reader's guide is a compiled list of resources and contains topics such as recommended reading, tips for parents and educators, a section on public speaking for introverts, and a conversation with Susan Cain.
- About the author

Marni's Notes: Cain's take on the Big Ideas Template is intellectual and thought provoking. She hopes to shift our collective thinking on what it means to be an introvert. Packed with stories, research, and insights from a historical perspective, Cain brings us face to face with our flawed thinking when it comes to cultural assumptions, norms, and ideals.

EXAMPLE 2

Thrive: The Third Metric to Redefining Success and Creating a Life of Well-Being, Wisdom, and Wonder
by Arianna Huffington

Front Matter (The Setup)

- Praise for *Thrive*
- Dedication

- Table of contents
- Preface
- Introduction
  - o Defining the problem → the bad news. We are an exhausted, overworked society often lacking in meaningful connection, living in a constant state of hurry, and there never seems to be enough time.
  - o Defining your idea → the good news (or, why read the book). By embracing the ideas of, and redefining the way you see, well-being, wisdom, wonder, and giving, you can create a life that is far more fulfilling spiritually and emotionally.
  - o A call to action: Huffington hopes that the reader will reconnect with themselves, their loved ones, and their community—and, therefore, thrive.

Body Matter (Core Content of the Book)

- Part One: Well-Being
- Part Two: Wisdom
- Part Three: Wonder
- Part Four: Giving
- Epilogue

End Matter (Optional Wrap-up Materials at the Back of the Book)

- Appendices
- Acknowledgments
- Notes
- Index
- About the author

Marni's Notes: Huffington's take on the Big Ideas Template is simple and clean. She strives to shift our collective thinking when it comes to four big concepts: Well-Being, Wisdom, Wonder, and Giving. She allows the reader a behind-the-scenes glimpse into her own life, as a guide for what can go wrong when one lives with exhaustion, stress, and lack of sleep. Including quotes and stories from a myriad of thinkers, Huffington shares how she broke out of this mold, to uncover a healthier, happier way of existing, and explains how you too can thrive.

EXAMPLE 3

Playing Big:
Practical Wisdom for Women
Who Want to Speak Up, Create, and Lead
by Tara Mohr

Front Matter (The Setup)

- Praise for *Playing Big*
- Dedication
- Table of contents
- Introduction
  - Defining the problem → the bad news. Often, brilliant women can't see their brilliance, and, much of the time, they play small.
  - Defining your idea → the good news (or, why read the book). There is a way to believe in yourself, tap into your brilliance, and allow yourself to shine—yes, you can learn to play big.
  - My Story: how Mohr came to write this book
  - About the book (where the material comes from and what you will find in the book overall).
  - A call to action for the reader, a call to turn the page. Mohr hopes that by reading the book, the reader will

tap into their inner brilliance and find the courage to change the world by sharing their gifts.

Body Matter (Core Content of the Book)

- Chapter 1: The Inner Critic
- Chapter 2: The Voice of Inner Wisdom
- Chapter 3: A Very Old New Way of Looking at Fear
- Chapter 4: Unhooking From Praise and Criticism
- Chapter 5: Leaving Good-Student Habits Behind
- Chapter 6: Hiding
- Chapter 7: Leaping
- Chapter 8: Communicating with Power
- Chapter 9: Callings
- Chapter 10: Let It Be Easy
- Conclusion: Joining the Transition Team

End Matter (Optional Wrap-up Materials at the Back of the Book)

- Afterword
- Acknowledgments
- Notes and sources

Marni's Notes: Mohr's take on the Big Ideas Template is motivational and inspirational. She acts as a guide to help the reader travel inward, examine how she currently sees herself, and face down old fears and beliefs. Mohr offers gentle but powerful insight that challenges every woman to stop playing small and selling ourselves short. Her goal is to shift our collective thinking toward feeling both inspired and empowered in order to realize our full potential.

Big Ideas Template Chapter Recipes

We zoomed out and looked at the overall structure for books that use the Big Ideas Template. Now we are going to zoom in and look at the various ways a writer can craft her chapters.

Chapter recipes for the Big Ideas Templates can vary; thus, you can be highly creative here. Remember: Anchors are elements you will see in every chapter. Variables are specific to that chapter.

 Anchors help to create a solid chapter structure.

 Variables provide variety and eye-catching interest.

Just like your book, chapters have personalities. Ask, *how can the personality of your chapters reflect the personality of your book?*

Build-Your-Own-Chapter

Chapters for the Big Ideas Template tend (and I do mean *tend*, because there are no hard-and-fast rules here) to have four sections.

📷 A QUICK SNAPSHOT: THE FOUR PARTS OF A CHAPTER FOR THE BIG IDEAS TEMPLATE

1. Introduction	→	Here's the Idea
2. Discussion	→	What the World Thinks About the Idea
3. Support	→	Why I See the Idea This Way
4. Conclusion	→	As We Leave This Idea, Think About This

The Parts of the Big Ideas Template Chapter

- **Introduction of an Idea:** *Here's the Idea*
  (Select one or more from below)
    - What we are going to talk about today is …
    - How the author views an idea
    - Story
    - Quotes/question or excerpt
    - Visual aid: infographics/charts/drawings/graphics/ pictures

- **Discussion of the Idea:** *What the World Thinks About the Idea* (Select one or more from below)
    - Strengths and weaknesses of the idea (the good, the bad, and the ugly)
    - How society sees the idea
    - How the author sees the idea (or how the author views society's take on the idea)
    - Self-assessment quizzes
    - Stories, vignettes, or case studies
    - Quotes or excerpts
    - Worksheets/questions/opportunities to journal
    - Research/historical information/statistics
    - Tools/practices/exercises
    - Prayers/meditations/affirmations
    - Visual aid: infographics/charts/drawings/graphics/ pictures
    - Plan-of-action/system/steps
    - Bulleted or numbered lists

- **Support for the Author's Point of View on the Idea:** *Why I See the Idea This Way*
  (Select one or more from below)
    - Stories, vignettes, or case studies
    - Quotes or excerpts
    - Worksheets/questions/opportunities to journal

- o Research/historical information/statistics
- o Tools/practices/exercises
- o Prayers/meditations/affirmations
- o Visual aid: infographics/charts/drawings/graphics/ pictures
- o Bulleted or numbered lists

- **Conclusion:** *As We Leave This Idea, Think About This* (Select from below)
  - o Brief summary or summary with insight
  - o Question or transitional hook
  - o Visual aid: infographics/charts/drawings/graphics/ pictures
  - o Takeaways

WARNING: Even though they look sparkly, try not to go overboard with too many chapter ingredients.

Chapter Recipes: Examples From the Bookshelf

Let's return to the bookshelf and take a look at how our three "Big Ideas" authors, Susan Cain, Arianna Huffington, and Tara Mohr, chose to construct their chapters.

Example 1

*Quiet: The Power of Introverts in a World
That Can't Stop Talking*
by Susan Cain

Cain's chapters are highly intellectual, clean, and jam-packed with thought-provoking insights. She starts every chapter with a relevant quote. She offers a story that illuminates her chapter idea. What follows is a discussion of the story and its relevance to the main idea of the chapter. She then branches into a discussion of the chapter idea using a variety of supportive elements such as compelling personal stories, research, or historical perspective. She concludes each chapter with a summation or a question that makes you want to turn the page. Her chapters feel like talking with a super-smart friend that makes you reconsider all your previous ways of thinking about an issue.

Chapter Recipe for *Quiet*

- Quote
- Engaging story (personal or about a famous person, place, or moment in history) to introduce the chapter idea
- Discussion/analysis of the story, its meaning, its connection to the chapter idea
- Discussion of the chapter idea using a variety of the following
  - Bulleted-discussion points
  - Research, statistics, or case studies
  - Stories or vignettes
  - Mini self-assessments
  - Cultural history and background
- Summation with a compelling question or conclusion

 Anchors → Quote, story, analysis of story

 Variables → Supportive information for the main idea of the chapter, including stories, vignettes, statistics, and discussion points. The way Cain ends each chapter varies.

EXAMPLE 2

*Thrive: The Third Metric to Redefining Success and
Creating a Life of Well-Being, Wisdom, and Wonder*
by Arianna Huffington

Huffington offers long chapters that cover four master concepts of the book: Well-Being, Wisdom, Wonder, and Giving. She includes fun and interesting subheadings like *Sleep Your Way to the Top* (which is truly about sleep) and *Meditation: It's Not Just for Enlightenment Anymore*. Lots of quotes serve to support the subheadings and break up the chapters visually. She includes thoughts from a variety of thinkers including novelists, poets, clergy, psychology professors, researchers, entrepreneurs, and entertainers. She offers an interesting, behind-the-scenes look at her experiences and career, and how she has integrated these master concepts into her own life. Since the premise of the book is about slowing down and reconsidering what you deem important in your life, the chapters are not frenetic, nor do they offer eye-catching, magazine-style snippets. Her chapters feel more like taking a long walk with a calming friend, which allows you to (almost) meditate on the concepts.

Chapter Recipe for *Thrive*

- Opening quote that introduces the main concept (on its own page)
- Discussion of the concept—the good, the bad, and the ugly—and how Huffington sees the concept overall
- Discussion of the chapter idea using a variety of the following
    o Instructional steps (often what worked for Huffington herself)
    o Supportive stories
    o Bulleted lists
    o Statistical findings
    o Quotes
    o Poems
    o Writing excerpts from famous (and not-so-famous) thinkers
    o Personal stories
    o Cherokee legends

Anchors → Each new master concept begins with a relevant quote on its own page. On the next page, Huffington introduces her thinking on the master concept. Every chapter has lots of quotes sprinkled throughout.

Variables → Supportive information for the main idea, such as stories, instructional steps, poems, legends, excerpts, bulleted lists, and statistics. The chapter endings also vary.

EXAMPLE 3

Playing Big: Practical Wisdom for Women
Who Want to Speak Up, Create, and Lead
by Tara Mohr

Mohr's chapters are highly instructional, appealing to the eye with lots of white space and fun lists. She begins each chapter with an introduction of the main concept. She supports her ideas with a variety of interesting lists, charts, and quotes. She asks the reader to think deeper with journaling questions and creative exercises. The chapters are interactive as Mohr is often challenging us to look at our inner life in order to see ourselves in new and different ways. The subheading of the book promises "Practical wisdom for women who want to speak up, create, and lead," and the chapters deliver that concrete, actionable wisdom.

Chapter Recipe for *Playing Big*

- Introduction of the main concept or idea for the chapter
- Discussion of the main concept using a variety from below
  - Instructional steps
  - Supportive stories

- o Do's and don'ts
- o Bulleted and numbered lists
- o Quotes
- o Cognitive tools
- o Somatic tools
- o Personal stories
- o Journaling questions
- o Charts
- o Scripts
- o Checklists
- o Practices, creative exercises, and heart-based tools
- o Infographics
- o Self-guided visualizations
- o Big ideas (takeaways) at the end of the chapter

 Anchors → Introduction of the main concept at the beginning, journaling questions, and takeaways at the end of the chapter.

 Variables → Supportive information for the main idea, such as actionable tools, wisdom, infographics, and stories.

Bite-Sized Thoughts for Chapter 11

1. The Big Ideas Template is the most common and universal. Think: a big call to action that may require a shift in consciousness. If you use this template, your book will focus on a call for a new way of thinking, such as learning how to invigorate your soul, better understanding your body, awakening your inner genius, or learning how to face down fear.

2. With this template, the information is usually broken up into parts (or sections) with chapters underneath those parts. Usually, the first one or two chapters cover the overall theory, and the last chapter offers a summary, conclusion, and call to action.

3. Reviewing the way bestselling authors Susan Cain, Arianna Huffington, and Tara Mohr have crafted their books within the Big Ideas Template can help you to brainstorm ways in which you might bring your own book to life.

4. Here is a quick snapshot of the four parts of a chapter for the Big Ideas Template:

Introduction	→	Here's the Idea
Discussion	→	What the World Thinks About the Idea
Support	→	Why I See the Idea This Way
Conclusion	→	As We Leave This Idea, Think About This

The Big Ideas Template allows for a lot of creativity when crafting a chapter recipe. Meaning, you can integrate lots of interesting ways to support your ideas, such as stories, journaling questions, charts, and checklists. But be careful of adding too many chapter ingredients, as that can become overwhelming for the reader. Only use the ingredients that are helpful and essential.

CHAPTER 12

THE STORIES TEMPLATE

The Stories Template is filled with one big story or lots of little stories, vignettes, or reflections that illustrate the ideas or theory behind the book. It's a little lower on actionable steps. The stories are the star of the show.

Generally, this template is a jump-right-in kind of template. There is usually a minimal amount of front matter, and then we dive right into stories, reflections, lessons, or messages. The stories (or vignettes, lessons, or reflections) form the bulk of the book, and sometimes, the book contains little-to-no end matter.

The Parts of the Stories Template

Now, let's take a look at the front, body, and back matter of the Stories Template.

Front Matter

- Praise for
- Dedication
- Table of contents

- Introduction
  - Defining the issue or problem
  - How the stories, vignettes, or reflections address the issue
  - Why I wrote this book; a bit about me
  - A call to turn the page

Body Matter (Core Content of the Book)
If the Book Has Many Stories – Option A

- Parts/Sections/Chapters: in that order. You can break the material down into parts and sections if you want, or just chapters.
  - Chapter 1: Usually an exploration of the theme and story number one
  - Chapter 2: Story number two
  - Chapter 3: Story number three (and so on, until you have told all of your stories)
- Close → (Often a hope, wish, or call to action): A chapter that summarizes the material, offers an inspirational message that ties all the stories together, and restates the theme of the book. Can also offer a specific call to action or a call to join a community.

Body Matter (Core Content of the Book)
If the Book Focuses on One Big Story – Option B

- Parts/Sections/Chapters: in that order. You can break the material down into parts and sections if you want, or just chapters.
  - Chapter 1: Usually an exploration of the theme, and the story begins
  - Chapter 2: Story continues
  - Chapter 3: Story continues (and so on until you have completed your story)

- Close → (Often a hope, wish, or call to action)
    - A chapter that summarizes the material, offers an inspirational message that ties the story together, and restates the theme of the book. Can also offer a specific call to action or a call to join a community.

End Matter (Optional Materials at the Back of the Book)

- Afterword
- About the author
- Index
- Notes
- Chapter from next book (if included)
- Other optional end matter
    - Glossary
    - Appendix
    - Bibliography
    - Reader's guide
    - Recommended reading
    - Resources
    - Tips for parents or educators
    - Interview with the author

I am going to present you with three examples from the bookshelf that will show different ways of using the Stories Template. Oprah Winfrey's book, *The Wisdom of Sundays: Life-Changing Insights From Super Soul Conversations*, focuses not so much on stories, but more on reflections of spiritual concepts. The focus of Sophia Amoruso's *#GIRLBOSS* is to share the author's personal story as well as the stories of other inspirational girl bosses. Rachel Naomi Remen's book, *Kitchen Table Wisdom: Stories That Heal*, is probably the most classic version of the Stories Template, as hers is a collection of short stories organized by a unifying theme.

Q: When Is a Collection of Stories Just a Collection of Stories, and What Exactly Makes That Collection of Stories a Thought Leader Book?

A: Think of it this way: What is the clear intention of the book? If the intention is to entertain through funny stories, then it might be a collection of stories. If the intention is to provoke thought, add something significant to the cultural conversation, or offer new and unique information, then you most likely have a thought leader book.

Q: What If I Want to Use Many Stories From (or About) Different People?

A: Use Option A, *The Wisdom of Sundays* by Oprah Winfrey if you plan on using many stories (see Example 1).

Q: What If I Want to Focus on One Long Story and Break It Up Into Parts?

A: Use Option B, *#GIRLBOSS* by Sophia Amoruso if you plan on focusing mostly on one longer story (see Example 2).

The Stories Template: Examples From the Bookshelf

To gain a better understanding of the Stories Template, let's return to the bookshelf and look at some books that utilize this template.

Remember: These books are in the Stories Template because the stories themselves are the star of the show. Any other information, guidance system, or steps are the backup players.

EXAMPLE 1

The Wisdom of Sundays:
Life-Changing Insights From Super Soul Conversations
by Oprah Winfrey

(This is just a beautiful book to hold. It is filled with calming pictures of nature and sunlight.)

Front Matter

- Authors' Note (also serves as a kind of dedication or expression of gratitude for contributors)
- Introduction
  - Quote from Oprah
  - Defining the issue or problem: We are all seeking deeper meaning in life, and deeper connection to our truest expression of ourselves.
  - How the stories and photographs address the issue: Oprah collected some of the most powerful spiritual lessons and "aha moments" she had on her TV show, *SuperSoul Sunday*. She also includes photos of nature that are reminders of the "majesty abundance" open to all of us.
  - A call to action/call to turn the page: Oprah hopes that the *Wisdom of Sundays* not only illuminates our path but pushes us to become all that we are meant to be. She invites us to turn the page and enjoy the journey.

Body Matter (Core Content of the Book)
If the Book Has Many Stories – Option A

The meat of the book focuses on stories, snippets of interviews, and quotes, broken up into ten chapters of "aha moments" that Oprah has had with some of today's most admired thought leaders. Each piece of wisdom is set against a beautiful backdrop of inspirational photographs of nature.

- Chapter 1 – Awakening (Starts with a quote and reflection from Oprah)
    - Includes quotes, interviews, or reflections from thought leaders, including Carolyn Myss, Deepak Chopra, and Ram Dass.

- Chapter 2 – Intention (Starts with a quote and reflection from Oprah)
    - Includes quotes, interviews, or reflections from thought leaders such as Iyanla Vanzant, Brené Brown, and Sue Monk Kidd.

- Chapter 3 – Mindfulness (Starts with a quote and reflection from Oprah)
    - Includes quotes, snippets of interviews, or reflections from thought leaders such as Jon Kabat-Zinn, Shonda Rhimes, and Arianna Huffington.

- Chapter 4 – Spiritual GPS (Starts with a quote and reflection from Oprah)
    - Includes quotes, interviews, or reflections with thought leaders such as Cheryl Strayed, President Jimmy Carter, and Elizabeth Gilbert.

- Chapter 5 – Ego (Starts with a quote and reflection from Oprah)
    - Includes quotes, snippets of interviews, or reflections from thought leaders such as Wayne Dyer, Jack Canfield, and Pema Chödrön.

- Chapter 6 – Forgiveness (Starts with a quote and reflection from Oprah)
  - Includes quotes, snippets of interviews, or reflections from thought leaders such as Adyashanti, Mark Nepo, and Don Miguel Ruiz.

- Chapter 7 – Broken Open (Starts with a quote and reflection from Oprah)
  - Includes quotes, snippets of interviews, or reflections from thought leaders such as Gabrielle Bernstein, Glennon Doyle, and Dr. Shefali Tsabary.

- Chapter 8 – Grace and Gratitude (Starts with a quote and reflection from Oprah)
  - Includes quotes, snippets of interviews, or reflections from thought leaders such as Geneen Roth and Gretchen Rubin.

- Chapter 9 – Fulfillment (Starts with a quote and reflection from Oprah)
  - Includes quotes, snippets of interviews, or reflections from thought leaders such as Paulo Coelho, India Arie, and Shonda Rhimes

- Chapter 10 – Love and Connection (Starts with a quote and reflection from Oprah)
  - Includes quotes, snippets of interviews or reflections from thought leaders such as Maya Angelou, Malala Yousafzai, and Elie Wiesel.

- Close → Ends with a quote from Oprah

End Matter (Optional Materials at the Back of the Book)

The book concludes with an epilogue, acknowledgments, credits, a section on the contributors, and an about the author page.

- Epilogue
- Contributors
- About the author
- Credits and acknowledgments

EXAMPLE 2

#GIRLBOSS
by Sophia Amoruso

Amoruso infuses her style into all aspects of the book, including bold black pages with large white lettering, inky cartoons, personal pictures of her growing up, and bold and funny chapter titles. She travels back and forth between addressing her reader's wants and needs (to become a girl boss) with her own story, how she became the CEO and founder of NastyGal, a multi-million-dollar fashion company. Her stories, and her style, are the star of this show. This template comes close to being a memoir. The difference is that Amoruso's main focus is that her story can help the reader. She offers a life/business lesson for anyone that wants to become a #GIRLBOSS, and then she supports that lesson with stories from her own life experiences.

Front Matter

- Praise for *#GIRLBOSS*
- About the author
- Table of contents
- Introduction to the introduction
- Introduction
  - The chronology of a *#GIRLBOSS*
  - Defining the issue or problem: In eight years she went from a broke anarchist to a millionaire businesswoman.

o   How her life stories address the issue: She invites
the reader to learn from her mistakes, identify their
weaknesses, and play to their strengths.

o   A call to action/a call to turn the page: three pieces of
advice—to not ever grow up, become boring, or let
the man get to you.

Body Matter (Core Content of the Book)
If the Book Is One Big Story – Option B

- Chapter 1 – So You Want to Be a #Girlboss
- Chapter 2 – How I Became a #Girlboss
- Chapter 3 – Shitty Jobs Saved My Life
- Chapter 4 – Shoplifting (and Hitchhiking) Saved My Life
- Chapter 5 – Money Looks Better in the Bank Than on
Your Feet
- Chapter 6 – Hocus Pocus: The Power of Magical Thinking
- Chapter 7 – I Am the Antifashion
- Chapter 8 – On Hiring, Staying Employed, and Firing
- Chapter 9 – Taking Care of (Your) Business
- Chapter 10 – Creativity in Everything
- Chapter 11 – The Chances (This also acts as a conclusion
and a call to action—there is a chance for you, so take it!)

Notes on the body matter: The book reads like a combo of
a magazine and a girlfriend's guide to business success. Each
chapter begins with a stylized cartoon offering a sassy message,
and an offbeat quote. Amoruso includes quirky pictures of herself
growing up and into the woman she has become. She also includes
spotlight sections where she highlights other successful women,
calling them Portrait of a #Girlboss. These sections are written
by the successful businesswomen themselves, speaking directly to
the reader and expressing their take on being a #Girlboss.

End Matter (Optional Materials at the Back of the Book)

- Acknowledgments
- Invitation to connect
- One-page promo for her next book, *Nasty Galaxy*

EXAMPLE 3

Kitchen Table Wisdom: Stories That Heal
by Rachel Naomi Remen, MD

Remen begins the book with a preface, a foreword, and an introduction. The meat of the book is broken up into nine parts; each part contains between five and thirteen short stories, either about her life or about those that have touched her life. The book ends with an epilogue and acknowledgments.

Front Matter

- Praise for *Kitchen Table Wisdom*
- Table of contents
- Preface
- Foreword
- Introduction
  - Defining the issue or problem: Remen believes that "despite the awesome powers of technology, many of us still do not live very well."
  - How the stories address the issue: Remen believes that to live richer, more meaningful, and healthier lives, "we may need to listen to one another's stories again."
  - Why I wrote this book – a bit about me
  - A call to turn the page

Body Matter (Core Content of the Book)
If the Book Covers Many Stories – Option A

- Part 1: Life Force—Includes seven stories, with titles such as "Plum Blossoms" and "Silence"
- Part 2: Judgment—Includes thirteen stories, with titles such as "Back to Basics" and "Beyond Perfection"
- Part 3: Traps—Includes seven stories, with titles such as "Healing at a Distance" and "Lag Time"
- Part 4: Freedom—Includes five stories, with titles such as "Another Kind of Silence" and "Going Home"
- Part 5: Opening the Heart—Includes ten stories, with titles such as "Just Listen" and "To Be Seen by the Heart"
- Part 6: Embracing Life—Includes thirteen stories, with titles such as "At Last" and "Three Fables on Letting Go"
- Part 7: Live and Help Live—Includes eight stories, with titles such as "Live and Help Live" and "Healing is Mutual"
- Part 8: Knowing God—Includes eight stories, with titles such as "What if God Blinks" and "Consecrating the Ordinary"
- Part 9: Mystery and Awe—Includes eight stories, with titles such as "Seeing Around the Corner" and "Remembering the Sacred"
- Close: The Final Lesson

End Matter (Optional Materials at the Back of the Book)

- Epilogue
- Acknowledgments

Chapter Recipes: Examples From the Bookshelf

Let's take a look at how the authors of the Stories Template, Oprah Winfrey, Sophia Amoruso, and Rachel Naomi Remen, have organized their chapters. You may notice that the chapter recipes for the Stories Template are fairly simple. The focus is either on one big story, or the collection of stories and reflections. You may find an introduction to a concept, but overall, the reader is there to dive into the stories.

EXAMPLE 1

The Wisdom of Sundays:
Life-Changing Insights From Super Soul Conversations
by Oprah Winfrey

Oprah's chapter recipe is simple. Since the premise of the book is about slowing down and reflecting on life, the chapter recipe has an easy, meditative feel. Nothing is in your face—no statistics or bulleted lists. This book focuses on snippets of thoughts that provoke insight or awakening. Pictures of nature feature heavily into each chapter and help to create a calming and thought-provoking atmosphere. Oprah's chapters include four parts and do not include any sort of summary or conclusion.

Chapter Recipe for *The Wisdom of Sundays*

- Quote from Oprah to introduce the chapter idea. Picture of nature as background
- Oprah's personal reflection on the idea
- Collection of thought leaders' reflections on the idea or concept, with pictures of nature sprinkled throughout

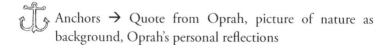 Anchors → Quote from Oprah, picture of nature as background, Oprah's personal reflections

Variables → Supportive information for the main idea, such as which thought leaders are highlighted in each chapter and where the pictures of nature are featured. Some pictures serve as background, while others stand alone.

EXAMPLE 2

#GIRLBOSS
by Sophia Amoruso

Amoruso's chapters have a fun, youthful feel to them. The premise of the book is about women owning their unique powers and running their own careers, and the chapters have a bold and quirky feel to them. She openly discusses her failures and successes and sprinkles her attitude around the book with ease. Her style is unapologetic, and her subheadings are funny. She includes attitude-filled pictures of herself at different stages in her life, along with humorous and stylish drawings. Her chapters feel like talking to an unconventional, highly successful friend who will share her real story, not the fake glossy story, about her path to success.

Chapter Recipe for *#GIRLBOSS*

- Drawing
- Quote on the chapter title page
- Discussion of idea
- Discussion of the chapter idea using a variety from below
  - Her story
  - Pictures
  - Quotes
  - Portraits of other girl bosses

Anchors → Drawing, quote on the chapter title page, quote at the end of the chapter

 Variables → Supportive information for the main idea, such as placement of stories, pictures, quotes, and portraits of other girl bosses.

EXAMPLE 3

Kitchen Table Wisdom:
Stories That Heal
by Rachel Naomi Remen, MD

The book is broken up into nine parts or nine main concepts (such as life force, traps, judgment, and freedom). When the author introduces the idea, she presents a story or a reflection about the concept. Stories follow, all discussing, in one form or another, the central idea. So, the chapter recipe is very simple.

Chapter Recipe for *Kitchen Table Wisdom*

- Author's reflection on the chapter idea/concept
- Series of short stories (between five and thirteen per chapter) that discuss, question, or illuminate the idea/concept

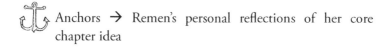 Anchors → Remen's personal reflections of her core chapter idea

 Variables → The number of stories per chapter

Bite-Sized Thoughts for Chapter 12

1. The focus of this template is on one big story or lots of little stories (or reflections) that illustrate the theory behind the book. The stories are the star of the show. For this template, writers usually dive right into stories. Often the book contains little-to-no front or end matter.

2. Reviewing the way bestselling authors such as Oprah Winfrey, Sophia Amoruso, and Rachel Naomi Remen have crafted their books within the Stories Template can help you to brainstorm ways in which you might bring your book to life.

3. If you want to utilize many stories from (or about) different people, study the structure of Option A, *The Wisdom of Sundays* by Oprah Winfrey. If you want to focus on one long story and break it up into parts, study the structure of Option B, *#GIRLBOSS* by Sophia Amoruso.

4. A collection of stories can be considered a thought leader book when the clear intention is to provoke thought, offer unique information, or add to the cultural conversation.

5. Chapter recipes for the Stories Template tend to be simple. There may be a brief introduction or closing, but overall, the reader is there to dive into the stories.

CHAPTER 13

THE PLAN-OF-ACTION TEMPLATE

The Plan-of-Action Template is highly actionable and offers clear advice for success. This template is effective if you have a clear program, a plan that involves steps, or an actionable method that answers a problem. The Plan-of-Action template is the most directive. If you tend to communicate your ideas using a specific plan to help people achieve a certain type of success, then this is the template for you.

The Parts of the Plan-of-Action Template

Front Matter

- Dedication
- Introduction
- Defining the issue: the bad news
- Solutions to the problem: the good news
- Why I wrote this book
- A call to turn the page

Body Matter (Core Content of the Book)

- Parts/Sections/Chapters—in that order. You can break the material down into parts and sections if you want, or just chapters. Often each chapter is a step.
  - Chapter 1: Step one
  - Chapter 2: Step two
  - Chapter 3: Step three (and so on, until you have covered all of your steps)

- Close → (Often a hope, wish, or call to action)
  - One or two chapters that summarize the material and offer a specific call to action or a call to join a community.

End Matter (Optional Materials at the Back of the Book)

- Afterword
- About the author
- Index
- Notes
- Chapter from next book (if included)

Q: Where Might a Plan-Of-Action Template Go Wrong?

A: If the system involves too many steps, or the steps are confusing, the reader may check out. To help retain engagement and follow through, explain your plan of action as simply as possible. Sometimes this involves rethinking your plan and eliminating unnecessary steps or parts.

Plan-of-Action Template: Examples From the Bookshelf

To gain a better understanding, let's return to the bookshelf and look at some books that follow the Plan-of-Action Template.

Remember: These books are in the Plan-of-Action Template because the focus of the book is on a system or series of steps that will help your reader to reach a specific outcome. The stories and other supportive information are the backup players.

EXAMPLE 1

Boss Bitch:
A Simple 12-Step Plan to Take Charge of Your Career
by Nicole Lapin

Front Matter

- Advance praise for *Boss Bitch*
- Dedication (to her former self!)
- Table of contents
- Quote
- Introduction
    - Defining the issue: Being a boss bitch is a good thing; it means owning your life and taking charge of your future.
    - Why I wrote this book
    - A call to turn the page

Body Matter (Core Content of the Book)

Section one has two steps, section two has five steps, and section three has five steps. The book ends with an acknowledgments section and a business dictionary.

- Section One: Being the Boss of You
    - Step 1: Owning the Boss Mentality
    - Step 2: Be the CEO of You

- Section Two: Being the Boss at Work
  - Step 1: Think Like a Boss
  - Step 2: Talk Like a Boss
  - Step 3: Be a Goal Digger
  - Step 4: You Better (Net)Work Bitch
  - Step 5: The View From the Top

- Section Three: Being the Boss of Your Own Business
  - Step 1: Every Day I'm (Side) Hustling
    - How to Explore Your Passions and Make Extra Money
  - Step 2: I'm not a Business (wo)man, I'm a Business, (Wo)man
    - Deciding Whether Your Own Business is Viable
  - Step 3: How the Heck Do You Start a Business, Anyway?!
    - The Nuts and Bolts of Getting Your Gig off the Ground
  - Step 4: Teamwork Makes the Dreamwork
    - #Winning with an All-Star Team
  - Step 5: Girls Just Wanna Have Funds
    - Making Money and Losing Money (Without Losing Yourself)
  - Closing section and wrap-up

End Matter (Optional Materials at the Back of the Book)

- The Business Dictionary (That You Don't Need a Dictionary to Understand)
- Acknowledgments
- Index

EXAMPLE 2

The 9 Steps to Financial Freedom:
Practical and Spiritual Steps So You Can Stop Worrying
by Suze Orman

Front Matter

- Preface (Her version of the introduction)
    - Defining the issue: Your future is at stake; it's time to take a look at what may scare you, and be the captain of your ship financially.
    - Defining the solution: Orman will teach you a new way to look at money to better understand that it is a state of mind. This shift can help you to bloom emotionally and financially.
    - Orman invites us to use this book to "embark on a course to financial freedom and true wealth."

- What Do You Want From Your Money? As a financial planner, Orman has learned what is behind most financial failures and has methods that can teach you how to view money to create a life of abundance.
    - The 9 Steps to Financial Freedom – A Preview
    - Setting Your Goals – Orman invites us to think about what we want to get out of this book (get out of debt, save for college, purchase a home, etc.)

Body Matter (Core Content of the Book)

- Step One: Seeing How Your Past Holds the Key to Your Financial Future

    Client vignettes, money messages, an exercise, a section called, "Think about your past"

- Step Two: Facing Your Fears and Creating New Truths

  Discussion of money fear, vignettes, questions, and exercises

- Step Three: Being Honest with Yourself

  Discussion of where your money truly goes, what is coming in and going out, an exercise, and a section on moving forward

  A Note on Steps 4, 5, and 6 (Orman prepares the reader for the next three steps)

- Step Four: Being Responsible to Those You Love

  Discussion about being responsible with money including wills and life insurance, the first law of financial freedom

- Step Five: Being Respectful of Yourself and Your Money

  Discussion of respect for yourself and your money, including 401Ks and retirement and debt and saving; the second, third, fourth, and fifth laws of financial freedom; an exercise; vignettes

- Step Six: Trusting Yourself More Than You Trust Others

  Discussion of trusting yourself, including feeling your financial pulse, worksheets, and finding financial advisors; the sixth law of financial freedom

  A Note on Steps 7, 8, and 9 (Orman prepares the reader for the next three steps)

- Step Seven: Being Open to Receive All That You Are Meant to Have

  An exercise, Orman's story, the reason to give

- Step Eight: Understanding the Ebb and Flow of the Money Cycle

  Orman's father's story, an exercise, inner knowing

- Step Nine: Recognizing True Wealth

  Vignette, an exercise

- Close → 9 Steps: A Review

  After a brief review, Orman wishes the reader abundance, joy, and true wealth—of all kinds.

End Matter (Optional Materials at the Back of the Book)

- Index
- About the author
- Also by Suze Orman

EXAMPLE 3

May Cause Miracles: A 40-Day Guidebook of Subtle Shifts
for Radical Change and Unlimited Happiness
by Gabrielle Bernstein

Front Matter

- Dedication
- Table of contents
- Introduction
  - Defining the issue: Many times in life, we allow a fear-mindset to rule over a miracle-mindset
  - Why I wrote this book: it's a choice you make, and you can choose to become a miracle maker
  - Overview of the 40-Day Plan

o A call to turn the page: let go, be guided, and expect miracles

Body Matter (Core Content of the Book)

Note: Each week is broken up into sections: Morning Reflection, Affirmation, and Evening Exercise. Some offer miracle moments and meditations.

- Week 1: Become Miracle Minded – Overview of the Week
  - o Day One – Witness Your Fear (morning reflection, affirmation, miracle moment, exercise)
  - o Day Two – Become Willing
  - o Day Three – Choose a New Perspective
  - o Day Four – Gratitude
  - o Day Five – Learning to Forgive
  - o Day Six – Expect Miracles
  - o Day Seven – Reflect and Prepare

- Week Two: A New Self-Perception
  - o Day Eight – Witness Your Self-Inflicted Fear
  - o Day Nine – Become Willing to Love Yourself
  - o Day Ten – Self Love
  - o Day Eleven – Self Gratitude
  - o Day Twelve – The F Word
  - o Day Thirteen – Go Big and Expect Miracles
  - o Day Fourteen – Reflect and Prepare

- Week Three: Body Image
  - o Day Fifteen – A New Reflection
  - o Day Sixteen – My Body is Light
  - o Day Seventeen – What Do I Choose to See in the Mirror
  - o Day Eighteen – Getting My Gratitude On!
  - o Day Nineteen – The Inverse of the Fog

- o Day Twenty – The Miracle of Your Body
- o Day Twenty-One – Reflect and Prepare

- Week Four: Relationships
  - o Day Twenty-Two – Witness Your Ego
  - o Day Twenty-Three – Be Willing to Turn Your Ego Over to Your -ING
  - o Day Twenty- Four – Kindness
  - o Day Twenty-Five – Be Grateful for the Purpose of the Relationship
  - o Day Twenty-Six – F Everyone!
  - o Day Twenty-Seven – Miraculous Relationships
  - o Day Twenty-Eight – Reflect and Prepare

- Week Five: Raise Your Self-Worth, Raise Your Net Worth
  - o Day Twenty-Nine – Witness Your Financial Fears
  - o Day Thirty – Willing to Change
  - o Day Thirty-One – A Financial Shift
  - o Day Thirty-Two – Gratitude Creates Abundance
  - o Day Thirty-Three – Finance and Forgiveness
  - o Day Thirty-Four – Money and Miracles
  - o Day Thirty-Five – Reflect and Prepare

- Week Six: Working Miracles
  - o Day Thirty-Six – Witness Your Ways in the World
  - o Day Thirty-Seven – Listen Up!
  - o Day Thirty-Eight – Shift From Me to We
  - o Day Thirty-Nine – Gratitude to the World
  - o Day Forty – A Letter of Forgiveness
  - o Day Forty-One – You Are a Miracle Worker
  - o Day Forty-Two – Reflect and Celebrate

- Conclusion: Living a Miraculous Life

End Matter (Optional Materials at the Back of the Book)

- Acknowledgments
- About the author

Chapter Recipes: Examples From the Bookshelf

Let's return to the bookshelf and take a look at how our authors for the Plan-of-Action Template created their chapter recipes.

You have a lot of options for your chapters in the Plan-of-Action Template. The basic recipe is introducing the step or lesson, then offering supporting information to explain and illuminate the step or lesson. To help you brainstorm, think about the feeling you are going for, or how you want your reader to feel as they flip through the pages. If the answer is calm and peaceful, then you may want a clean, meditative recipe. If the answer is energized and enthused, then you may want a chapter recipe that mixes it up, offering new and creative ways of presenting the information, like infographics and charts. If the answer is interactive and youthful, you may want your book to feel like a magazine with lots of images, self-assessment tests, and text boxes.

EXAMPLE 1

Boss Bitch:
A Simple 12-Step Plan to Take Charge of Your Career
by Nicole Lapin

Lapin's chapters are magazine-like. They are fun, entertaining, and visually interesting. She offers featured sections with fun subheadings. The feeling is bold, fun, and empowering, and her creative chapters reflect that feeling.

- Introduction of the step. The step is introduced, then illuminated, dissected, and discussed using a variety of the following

- o Personal stories (Confessions of a Boss Bitch)
- o Teaching tools
- o Lapin's insights
- o Bitch Tips/FYI sections
- o Infographics or charts
- o Vignettes or brief highlights, Confessions of a Boss Bitch
- o Scenarios, example dialogues
- o Lists
- o Do's and don'ts

- The Bottom Line (last page of the chapter, the takeaway section that reviews the conventional wisdom vs. the reality on the ground, where Lapin debunks the myths about business)

 Anchors → Introduction of the step, vignettes called, "Confessions of a Boss Bitch," The Bottom Line

 Variables → The supportive material, such as infographics, lists, charts, bitch tips, and example scenarios

EXAMPLE 2

The 9 Steps to Financial Freedom:
Practical and Spiritual Steps So You Can Stop Worrying
by Suze Orman

- Introduction of the Step. The step is introduced, then discussed and illuminated using the following
  - o Brief vignettes
  - o Thinking questions
  - o Exercises
  - o Laws of financial freedom
  - o Financial tools/worksheets

- o Orman's insights
- o Comparison charts
- o How to's (figure out a budget, set up a living trust, take stock of your credit, etc.)

Orman doesn't follow the same exact recipe for each step. She mixes it up, sometimes offering a story first, and then a concrete financial worksheet, followed by Orman's insights into the step. Sometimes, she starts off with a provocative question, dives into exercises, and a discussion of the laws of financial freedom. While she mixes it up, the basic recipe involves presentation of a step, then illumination of that step via vignettes, insights, and tools.

 Anchors → Presentation of the step, exploration of the step with examples and insights

 Variables → The supportive material such as when and where she places the vignettes, tools, worksheets, and charts

EXAMPLE 3

May Cause Miracles: A 40-Day Guidebook of Subtle Shifts
for Radical Change and Unlimited Happiness
by Gabrielle Bernstein

Bernstein organizes her chapters by day, so each day (of forty-two days) is a new chapter. She starts out with a brief thought on the goal for the day, and then offers a morning reflection, a daily affirmation, and an evening exercise. To punctuate (and elaborate on) different aspects of the reflections, affirmations, or exercises, Bernstein pulls in various supportive elements such as prayers, contemplative journaling questions, practices, and meditations. But overall, her chapter recipe is clean and clear.

Each Chapter Contains Four Parts:

1. Introduction of the idea/concept for the day
2. Morning Reflection
3. Daily Affirmation
4. Evening Exercise

Bernstein's conclusion chapter is the only chapter with a different recipe. She revisits all of the main ideas presented in the book, and reviews how to turn the principles into a daily practice. She ends with a call to action to live a miraculous life.

 Anchors → Introduction of the idea, Morning Reflection, Daily Affirmation, and Evening Exercise

 Variables → To support one of her main four-chapter ingredients, Bernstein offers up a variety of meditations, miracle moments, practices, prayers, examples of miracle-minded thinking, mantras, quotes, journaling questions, or closing thoughts.

Bite-Sized Thoughts for Chapter 13

1. The Plan-of-Action Template is effective if you have a program, plan, steps, or an actionable method. This template is the most action-oriented and directive.

2. Reviewing the way bestselling authors such as Nicole Lapin, Suze Orman, and Gabrielle Bernstein have crafted their books within the Plan-of-Action Template can help you to brainstorm ways in which you might bring your book to life.

3. Explain your Plan-of-Action as simply as possible. If it gets too confusing, readers may put the book down.

4. You have a lot of options for your chapters in the Plan-of-Action Template. The basic recipe is this

    - introduction of the step or lesson, then
    - supportive information to explain and illuminate the step or lesson.

5. To help you brainstorm your chapter recipe, think about the feeling you are going for, or how you want your reader to feel as they flip through the pages. If the answer is "calm and peaceful," then you may want a meditative recipe. If the answer is "energized," then you may want a chapter recipe that mixes it up, offering new and creative ways of presenting the information like infographics and charts.

CHAPTER 14

LOCATE THE SPARK THAT SETS YOUR TEMPLATE ON FIRE

Summersault, Tumble, or Skip to the Carpet

When my son entered kindergarten, it was highly encouraged that I join the Kinder-Mom Committee. I was told that said committee would guide me through all the brand-new information I would be receiving and help to prepare me for "my most successful parenting year ever!"

I agreed; I mean, of course, I wanted to have my most successful parenting year ever. Yet at the first meeting, I found I was beyond intimidated. These moms had it all under control. They had mom calendars, they had phone trees, they had volunteer badges, they even had complex, color-coded school calendars. They handed me a blank school calendar and a batch of colorful markers. One woman, let's call her Pam, noticed the lost look on my face. "I know," she said, "preschool was all fun and games and now you're in kindergarten. Your whole world has changed. But don't worry; all new kinder-moms go through the learning curve. You'll get it."

Pam meant business. She was the volunteer coordinator. I could tell she ran her home like an army barracks. She scared me. But I figured she was right. She had three boys; I only had one. All of her boys looked extremely well groomed, with beautiful hair and stylish shoes. She was never late. And Pam never found a dollop of oatmeal in her son's hair on the way to school.

So, it was time to put away our preschool silliness and hunker down. By my second Kinder-Mom Committee meeting, I too had a mom calendar. By my third meeting, I had a color-coded school calendar and I was part of the official phone tree. By the fourth meeting (despite working full-time), I was on the volunteer committee. I was a mess. Every morning, I woke up with the feeling that I was doing this whole kinder-mom thing wrong.

Tracy, one of my friends (who had known me since high school), looked at all of my color-coding, phone-tree, mom-organization and said, "Ummm, who are you and what have you done with Marni?"

I said, "I know it's a lot, but it's what you have to do to be a kinder-mom." I was determined to get it right. I knew that if I could just learn all the rules, I could master this brand-new world.

Pam suggested I take the early volunteer shift to help the teacher with the morning story-time routine. The day came to start volunteering in the classroom. After I got my volunteer badge, I proudly walked over to the classroom where my son was playing with his best friend, Ethan. Pam called me over, a concerned look on her face. "There is a reason I wanted you to take this particular volunteer shift," she said.

"Oh yeah? How come?"

"Well, there has been some concerning behavior. By your son, I mean."

"Oh no," I said. "What is he doing? What's wrong?"

Preparing to tell me disappointing news, Pam shook her head. "Your son," she said, "well, see, when it's morning story time, and all the kids meet at the circular rainbow rug, well, all the other kids, they follow the rules and walk calmly to the carpet."

"Uh-huh," I said.

"And, well, your son, you see, he summersaults to the carpet."

"He what?" I asked. Kind of amused.

"Yeah, I wanted to tell you before the teacher pulled you aside and embarrassed you. He summersaults to the carpet. And his behavior is influencing others. Yesterday, I saw Ethan copying him."

"Were they laughing?"

"Yes, they were," she said, shaking her head.

And then it all became clear. I swear it was at that moment, looking at her grimacing face, that the sun shone through the windows and bathed me in the light of relief. I felt a sudden rush of giddiness, like a sense of returning to myself. My lord, I had been twisting myself into parenting pretzels to be this wonder mom I thought I was supposed to be. But it wasn't me. Not at all.

I looked up at Pam, who was waiting for me to scold my son. Instead, I nodded and said, "Do you think he will show me?" and I left her. Mouth open, confused.

I walked over to my son. "Hey, Ben, Ethan, show me how you guys get to the carpet."

Laughing with pure joy they did a few summersaults and then sat quietly on their assigned spaces.

I got down on the floor. I asked the boys to show me. And I summersaulted along with them. They reminded me to tuck in my chin and hold my legs in tight. And it was just so much fun. I had forgotten how much fun summersaulting could be.

Pam looked on in horror. I stood up, smiled, and thanked her for her concern and told her I was quitting the Kinder-Mom Committee. On my way to the car, I tossed the color-coded calendar into the trash.

As I drove home, I laughed in relief. My son and his summersaulting ways had shown me I had to do this parenting thing in a way that felt right for me, for us. I knew that my way was softer, gentler, and filled with an occasional summersault.

I tell you this story because, yes, I want you to understand how books are constructed. Yes, I want you to present your ideas to the world in a way that is clear and coherent. I have edited enough books to know just how much organization counts. And I know, you—as a strong, accomplished woman—want to know the rules and do it all right.

But if you happen to be approaching writing the way I initially approached parenting, thinking that all you had to do was forget all of your intuition and learn all the "right" rules, I'm here to tell you that rules and organization alone do not create the magic. YOU, sharing how YOU see the world, that is the magic. You are what will make your book fly off the shelves.

So, if you want to summersault to the carpet, do it.

Connect With Your Purpose

Now that you have thought through how you want to organize your ideas, **I want you to connect to that part of you that had the desire to write your book in the first place. Locate that initial spark.**

Why do I ask you to find that initial spark? Often, right next to that spark, you will be able to feel the spirit of the book. Yes, it's true, every book has its own spirit. What happens when you connect to the spirit of the book is that you are tapping into an energy that your readers will feel. For example, right now, I am infusing a certain energy into my words. The energy I hope you are feeling is this

Take risks, my friend.

Allow yourself to be seen—you are worthy of that much light.

Allow for vulnerability—yes, you are still quite lovable.

And guess what? It's okay to tear up your color-coded calendar and summersault to the carpet from time to time.

Journal Moment

Grab your journal and don't hold back. Allow everything to bubble up to the surface.

Use this prompt.

The reason I am so passionate about my book is because _____

_____

_____

_____

_____

If the spirit of the book were talking to me right now, it would say

_____

_____

_____

_____

Once you have gotten all your thoughts down on paper, ask yourself, *is that original spark in my book? Is my passion showing?* If not, ask yourself, *how can I add more of that energy to my book?*

Q: What If I Can't Connect to That Place of Original Inspiration?

A: Many times, getting quiet helps. This can be difficult for busy, on-the-go women. A friend of mine is struggling with breast cancer. She is a fierce mama bear and a go-get-'em type. She recently shared with me how hard it is to have to slow down. I asked if maybe there was a message in the slowing down.

I shared with her about a time I was told I needed to be on bed rest. I was several months pregnant, running a brand-new program for youth-at-risk, with twenty-four kids on my roster, and the sole breadwinner for my family (my husband was in law school). And guess what? I did not think I could slow down.

The next day, I got into a car accident, running right into a literal STOP sign. When I looked up from the crash, there was a big sign on my windshield that said STOP. Usually, the universe is a lot subtler. But since I'm stubborn, I needed a huge stop sign in my windshield to slow me down.

I went to bed. And I hated it. Yet, in the stillness, something was able to bubble to the surface. In the stopping, I was forced to go within in a way I hadn't for a long time. And what started to pour out of me was a new writing voice, one that had been waiting to express itself but simply could not, because I had allowed it no space.

So, consider me your personal STOP sign.

Take some time, now, on purpose, to slow down, to go within and listen to what you have to say. The spirit of the book may just be talking to you.

Every day, before each writing session, take a moment to meditate, or pray, or center yourself in your magic. Connect to the feistiest, fiercest part of yourself, and allow her to take the pen.

Bite-Sized Thoughts for Chapter 14

1. Get silent; go deep to get big.

2. Take risks. A lot of them.

3. Make sure your passion is showing.

4. There is magic in you.

5. Summersault to the rainbow carpet. It's fun.

CHAPTER 15

HEY, WHAT ABOUT MY TITLE?

Note: This is a mostly made-up story, but I've watched it go down like this, something like a thousand times. So, it happens. A lot.

Mira had worked on her book for over four years. It was about creating a new kind of business school, one that could meet the expectations and needs of today's youth. Mira worked tirelessly. She interviewed leaders in her field, gathered statistics, and used her twenty-plus years of working at a business school to create a well-thought-out, brilliantly written book, calling for a change to her beloved-but-outdated business school system.

Mira was a little burned out by the end of her four-year writing process, and she decided to have a good friend pick the title and do the cover. When her book was complete, Mira headed to a finance conference. She was excited that Pamela, a highly respected finance professor and her personal idol, would be speaking there. After Pamela's presentation, Mira approached and excitedly told Pamela about the concept of her book. Pamela looked interested and said she was intrigued by the idea. They engaged in a five-minute discussion of her thesis. Then Mira reached into her bag and handed over her book. Mira watched as her idol's face plummeted. She looked at Mira with a mix of pity and annoyance, and politely exited. Mira followed up with Pamela by email four weeks later, then eight weeks later. It seemed Pamela never got around to cracking open her book.

The next month, Mira sat down with a branding expert. She took out her book and was met with a bit of a gasp. The branding expert said to her, "I hate to be the one to tell you this, but it looks like the cover was made in a week by a fourth grader."

Mira worked with the branding expert to come up with a stronger title and a professional cover.

The next year, Mira applied to speak at the finance conference. There she sold her book with her new cover and title. During the midday break, when many were ambling around looking over books, Pamela walked by and stopped to look at Mira's book. Mira pitched the concept and said they had met before. Pamela said she didn't quite remember, but she was excited to buy the book and read more. Pamela then paid for Mira's book and went off to teach her class. The next day during a break, Mira saw Pamela sipping coffee and reading *her* book. It was a lesson on just how much damage a bad title and unprofessional cover can do to a brilliant book.

They can't get to all that juicy-good information if they don't open the book.

Note: If you publish traditionally, you will not have input on the cover; they take care of that. If you publish with a hybrid publisher, you may or may not have any creative input on the cover. Make sure to ask that question, if being a part of cover design is important to you.

Note on the note: If you are not a designer, let the experts take over. Go with a reputable company or designer, express your ideas, but then allow them to do what they do best. By that I mean, sometimes we, writers, have no idea what a good cover should look like.

Here's the Deal With Titles

Titles must perform multiple tasks. They must evoke an emotion, create curiosity, or promise something truly unique. In this chapter, we will cover the ways in which a title can provoke, spark, or inspire a reader to pick up your book.

Sometimes you know your title right from the beginning. Sometimes a brilliant, concise, powerful title drops from the sky and into your lap—easy peasy, lemon squeezy. And then, sometimes, not so much. Sometimes, you struggle with the title. You play with words and phrases and still cannot come up with something that you feel captures the essence of your book.

Also, and this is important:

Sometimes Titles Come Last

If you are writing your first draft, don't worry about the title. The best title may arrive while writing the book itself. A phrase may pop out at you just after you have written it and, bam, there it is. Know that it's perfectly fine to use "Working Title" while you are writing. (This is so common in the writing world that there is a movie company called, "Working Title.")

Before we dissect what makes a good title, I want to take you through a little exercise.

Take a moment to look over these 160-plus real titles by female authors (without their subtitles). I chose to show you this many titles to mimic the experience that a prospective reader will go through when searching for a book. The typical reader is bombarded with hundreds of titles and often decides which one to buy within a few seconds.

Take a moment to skim the titles, and then ask,

Which titles am I drawn to? Why?

160-Plus Titles From the Bookshelf

Knowing Your Value	*Lean In*
How to Break Up with Your Phone	*#GIRLBOSS*
Sugar Crush	*Big Magic*
Broken Open	*Thrive*
The Metabolism Plan	*You Are a Badass*
Free Women, Free Men	*Presence*
I Don't Wait Anymore	*The Four Tendencies*
Quiet	*When Things Fall Apart*
May Cause Miracles	*Diary of a Mad Housewife*
Outrageous Acts and Everyday Rebellions	*Unlimited*
The New Fat Flush Plan	*Girls and Sex*
100 Days of Real Food	*How to Have a Good Day*
Women, Food, and Desire	*Option B*
I Thought It Was Just Me (But It Isn't)	*Playing Big*
The Happiness Project	*The Universe Has Your Back*
Empowering Women	*Daring Greatly*
Bad Feminist	*The Money Therapist*
The Wisdom of Sundays	*Woman Hollering Creek and Other Stories*
The Life-Changing Magic of Tidying Up	*Feminism Is for Everybody*
My Stroke of Insight	*The Pre-Diabetes Diet Plan*
A Woman's Way Through the Twelve Steps	*Appetites*
We're Going to Need More Wine	*Shrill*
The Highly Sensitive Person	*The 10-Day Belly Slimdown*
100 Days to Brave	*The Fast Metabolism Diet*

The Plan

No Mexicans, Women,
or Dogs Allowed

10-Day Green
Smoothie Cleanse

You Can Heal Your Life

Twelve Steps to a
Compassionate Life

The Beauty Myth

Clean Eating

Breaking Free From
Emotional Eating

Devotions From the Garden

Wild Women, Wild Voices

Living Juicy

The Not So Subtle Art
of Being a Fat Girl

The Origins of Totalitarianism

Love Warrior

Five Days at Memorial

The Sixth Extinction

Hospital

Dark Matter
and the Dinosaurs

The Glass Universe

The 10-Day Plan to
Nourish and Glow

Selling Anxiety

Change Your Life
Without Getting Out of Bed

Help, Thanks, Wow

Men Explain Things to Me

No Excuses

The Woman Warrior

The Brain Boost Diet Plan

Bird by Bird

In Search of
Our Mothers' Gardens

Are You There, Vodka?
It's Me, Chelsea

Never Threaten to
Eat Your Co-Workers

So Long, Insecurity

I Feel Bad About My Neck

So You Want to
Talk About Race

The New Jim Crow

This Won't Hurt a Bit

Storm in a Teacup

Hardball for Women

This Close to Happy

Slouching Towards Bethlehem

How to Be a Bawse

Women in Tech

8 Steps to a Pain-Free Back

I Choose Me

Women Who
Run With the Wolves

Unfinished Business

Ain't I a Woman

*Stop Dressing Your
Six-Year-Old Like as Skank*

*The Earth, My Butt, and
Other Big Round Things*

In the Company of Women

*Well-Behaved Women
Rarely Make History*

The Vagina Monologues

Working with Difficult People

*Sippy Cups Are
Not for Chardonnay*

This Messy Magnificent Life

Break Your Own Rules

Year of Yes

Loving What Is

*Nice Girls Don't Get t
he Corner Office*

Women Who Worry Too Much

How Women Mean Business

*Flying Lessons
and Other Stories*

Finding Your Own North Star

The Body Keeps the Score

It's OK That You're Not OK

On Life After Death

Ready to Be a Thought Leader?

Leave Me Alone, I'm Reading

Carry On, Warrior

The Gifts of Imperfection

Women Rocking Business

Bonk

The Artist's Way

How Remarkable Women Lead

Secrets of Six-Figure Women

Eat Mangoes Naked

How Women Rise

Power Through Partnership

The Road to Wealth

A History of God

*One Day My Soul
Just Opened Up*

Jesus Feminist

*Overcoming Fear,
Worry, and Anxiety*

Even God Is Single

Let it Shine More

*The Emotionally
Healthy Woman*

Hidden Figures

*Women, Spirituality and
Transformative Leadership*

Women & Power

*I Still Miss My Man:
But My Aim Is Getting Better*

And Still I Rise

The Myth of the Nice Girl

Educated	*This Will Be My Undoing*
Make Trouble	*Not That Bad*
You Do You	*Fear of Flying*
A Return to Love	*Codependent No More*
No Logo	*Mad Woman on the Loose*
The Path of Transformation	*Healing After Loss*
The Confidence Code	*Girl, Wash Your Face*
I Am Malala	*I Shouldn't Be Telling You This*
Nice Girls Don't Get Rich	*Successful Women Think Differently*
Radical Acceptance	*Before the Change*
It's Never Too Late to Begin Again	*We Should All Be Feminists*
Reading Lolita in Tehran	*Against Interpretation and Other Essays*
Silent Spring	*Household Education*

Take a moment to jot down the titles that stayed with you and why. Was it the topic? The attitude or humor of the author? The promise of new and interesting information? Did you feel like the author knew you or "got" you?

Here's a free-write prompt.

I was drawn to those titles because _____

_____

_____

_____

_____

Here's how some readers answered the prompt, *I was drawn to those titles because*

> "I am drawn to anything with a plan. I want to know that there is something concrete that I can do, steps I can follow. Nothing too loose. Just tell me what to do, and that it has worked before."

> "I just like funny titles. It makes me feel like the author gets me. Like she is my friend, and we are going to crack each other up. I love that feeling."

> "They are a bit in your face. I don't really have time to mess around at this point in my life. If I am going to take the time to read something, it should be bold, to the point. These titles sort of shouted out to me."

> "They make me feel like they are going to spark my imagination, maybe have fun and interesting stories that I can get lost in. I am so busy thinking all the time, I want my reading to be full of imagination and wonder."

Journal Opportunity

Looking over the titles you were drawn to, ask:

How did those titles make me feel? _____

_____

_____

_____

Did they spark any emotion or primal feeling in me like hope, excitement, or curiosity? _____

_____

_____

Did I feel a kinship with the author? _____

_____

_____

_____

Which titles turned me off? _____

_____

_____

_____

_____

_____

_____

_____

What's in a Good Title? Using the Three-Key Method to Help Us Out

Good titles deliver on the Three Keys: the Promise, Premise, and Approach. The best ones are clear and memorable, and they reveal the voice of the author.

Titles and the Three Keys

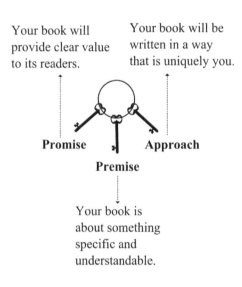

Your book will provide clear value to its readers.

Your book will be written in a way that is uniquely you.

Promise

Approach

Premise

Your book is about something specific and understandable.

Let's look at a few examples of some of my favorite titles.

Here is what a reader can glean, just by reading the following titles—nothing else.

EXAMPLE 1

Women Who Run with the Wolves:
Myths and Stories of the Wild Woman Archetype
by Clarissa Pinkola Estés, PhD

Promise: A part of you that you may not be connected to, or you would like to be more connected to, will be reawakened by reading stories and myths that capture a true and fierce feminine nature.

Premise: This book is filled with stories, fairy tales, and myths that describe something fierce and passionate that lives inside every woman.

Approach: The author's voice will be illuminating, inspirational, and empowering. The words will be feisty and sparkling with the lore of incredible women.

EXAMPLE 2

Men Explain Things to Me
by Rebecca Solnit

Promise: If you have ever felt a conversation with a man veer into some awkwardly condescending territory, you are not alone.

Premise: The author will discuss her observations and insights from her experience as a woman in today's society, where sometimes there is an assumption that women are not knowledgeable.

Approach: The author's voice will be direct, to the point, and sharp-witted. Her insights will be topical and thought-provoking.

EXAMPLE 3

How to Break Up with Your Phone:
The 30-Day Plan to Take Back Your Life
by Catherine Price

Promise: This book will help awaken you to your phone addiction and teach you how your constant interaction with your phone may be harming you, but also how you can learn a new way of coexisting.

Premise: This book will provide you with a practical 30-day plan to have a new, healthier connection to your most treasured technology.

Approach: The author's voice will be informative, actionable, and concrete—and, probably, a little funny too.

Q: Hey, Marni, Should My Title Reflect the Template I Have Chosen?

A: Yes, your title often reflects the template you have chosen. Here are some examples from the bookshelf, according to each template:

Ten "Big Ideas" Titles

The Universe Has Your Back

Wild Women, Wild Voices

When Things Fall Apart

Daring Greatly

Living Juicy

Secrets of Six-Figure Women

Women, Food, and Desire

Selling Anxiety

How Women Mean Business

Knowing Your Value

Ten "Stories" Titles

Chicken Soup for the Soul:
The Empowered Woman

Memories in Dragonflies:
Simple Lessons for Mindful Dying

Women Who Run with the Wolves

Good Night Stories for Rebel Girls: 100 Tales of
Extraordinary Women

Men Explain Things to Me

A Year Full of Stories:
52 Folk Tales and Legends From Around the World

Flying Lessons & Other Stories

Woman Hollering Creek and Other Stories

Let it Shine: Stories of Black Women Freedom Fighters

Girls Think of Everything:
Stories of Ingenious Inventions by Women

Ten "Plan-of-Action" Titles

The Metabolism Plan

8 Steps to a Pain-Free Back

The New Fat Flush Plan

100 Days to Brave

10-Day Green Smoothie Cleanse

May Cause Miracles

The Pre-Diabetes Diet Plan

12 Steps to a Compassionate Life

The 10-Day Plan to Nourish and Glow

100 Days of Real Food

What's in a Subtitle?

I don't mean to belittle subtitles by taking my sweet time getting to them. I think subtitles can save us all. Subtitles explain a bit more about the concept of your book. They can highlight essential information, so your reader knows if it's a book for her, and they can even assist in helping your book to be discovered online.

Sometimes a title is intriguing enough for the reader to pick it up, but not clear enough for the reader to make the purchase. Ah, here comes the subtitle to the rescue.

Subtitles Can

- Clarify
- Educate
- Define
- Excite
- Promote curiosity
- Extend the hand of the author
- Provoke
- Hook

Let's look at a few books with their subtitles attached. Note how the subtitles tell us more about the book and create a sense of curiosity or excitement.

- *The Conquer Kit: A Creative Business Planner for Women Entrepreneurs*
- *The Freedom Writers Diary: How a Teacher and 150 Teens Used Writing to Change Themselves and the World Around Them*
- *Sister Citizen: Shame, Stereotypes, and Black Women in America*
- *No Excuses: Nine Ways Women Can Change How We Think About Power*
- *Presence: Bringing your BOLDEST SELF to your BIGGEST Challenges*

Great Subtitles

> **Do** entice and lead
> **Don't** overexplain or confuse

What If No Title Is Coming to Me?

I want to remind you that it is completely normal to figure out your title at the tail end of the process. But if you are ready for your title, and nothing is coming—I offer you this:

Brainstorm, Brainstorm, Test, Test, Test

For the harder-to-find titles, you will want to brainstorm and test the title out, then repeat if necessary.

I will take you through four brainstorming exercises. Allow your mind to run free, maybe to places you didn't expect to go right away. Then test it out. Test it out with friends, family, your writing group, professional groups, Facebook groups, mastermind groups, dog groups, cat groups, and all other groups. People love to be part of a test campaign. You will get lots of opinions, but you will also begin to see which titles grab attention, spark imagination, and speak to your reader.

Note about testing out the title: Only ask people who want you to succeed. Your judgmental Aunt Edna is probably not the best test audience.

Brainstorm 1: Get to Know the Playing Field

Do your research. Look over titles of books that are similar to yours. Notice the ones you are drawn to and the ones you would never pick up. Familiarize yourself with the playing field. Pay attention to the words they use in their titles. Which words call to you? Write down the top three books that are in some way similar to yours and then circle the words you are drawn to

1. _____

   _____

2. _____

   _____

3. _____

   _____

Brainstorm 2: Personality

Ask: What word (or words) would you choose to describe the personality of your book? Examples include:

Feisty	Insightful
Educational	Bold
Intellectual	Healing
Calming	Transformative
Thought-provoking	Snarky
Spiritual	Informative
Funny	In-your-face
Fierce	(choose your own word)
Supportive	_____

Let's look at the book, *Well-Behaved Women Seldom Make History* by Laurel Thatcher Ulrich. Just based on the title, I would say that the book's personality is both feisty and intellectual.

Take a moment to free-write some words that describe the personality of your book

_____

_____

_____

_____

_____

Brainstorm 3: Feeling

What kind of emotions or what kind of experience should your book evoke? Ask: When they pick up my book, what do I want my reader to feel?

Dreamy	Silly
Challenged	Provoked
Hopeful	Wild
Interested	Supported
Curious	Enticed
Joyful	Happy
Relaxed	Excited
Smart/educated	Creative
Comforted	Empowered
Supported	(choose your own word)
Intrigued	_____

Let's look at the book, *Broken Open: How Difficult Times Can Help Us Grow* by Elizabeth Lesser. Just by reading the title, the feeling I get is that I will be comforted, and that I will gain a sense of hope. What feeling do you get just by reading the title?

Free write: I want my book/title to provoke these emotions

_____

_____

_____

_____

_____

A space to play: Using all of that juicy-good brainstorming, take a moment to play around, toying with different options for titles

_____

_____

_____

_____

_____

_____

_____

_____

_____

_____

_____

_____

Brainstorm 4: Electric Words

We first discussed electric words in Chapter 8 when we talked about summing up your idea. Pull out those words or brainstorm some new ones. For our purposes here, the electric words must be in the title or subtitle because they communicate the essence of your book, and they contain an authentic energy.

For example, let's look at the book, *Breaking Free From Emotional Eating* by Geneen Roth. The electric words are "emotional eating," as this concept is the core idea of the book. Roth could have chosen other initial words, like "stop" emotional eating or "how to eliminate" emotional eating. But "emotional eating" are two of her electric words, and most likely had to be in the title.

Examples of electric words: women, money, health, sleep, plan, boss, create, steps, guide, magic, power, growth, success, wisdom, worth, how-to, happiness, sanity, secrets, more, entrepreneur, work, leadership, healing, wholehearted, change, healing, control, big.

Take a moment to review or brainstorm some electric words that you think belong in your title. (Don't think too much here.)

Free write: Electric words for my title _____

_____

_____

_____

_____

_____

Test, Test, Test

When a new author comes to me with a working title, I like to take them through a series of questions called, the "title test." By looking through the lens of the Three Keys, we can see if the title is hitting or missing the mark. Remember that your title doesn't have to do everything, but it should be strong in several areas. The title test helps you figure out if you have a strong title or if you need to keep brainstorming.

The Title Test

Key #1: Promise

Does the title tell the reader what I am promising, or describe the clear value they will receive if they read my book?

Key #2: Premise

Does the title describe the core concept of the book?

Key #3: Approach

Does the title communicate my style?

Does the title promote kinship?

Is the title memorable?

Is the title relatively short or easy to say?

Bonus Question

Does the title communicate dynasty potential or journal potential?

Dynasty potential = the ability to write specialized offshoots or have a companion journal. For example, *Chicken Soup for the Soul* has been able to create specialized offshoots with titles such as *Chicken Soup for the Teenage Soul: 101 Stories of Life, Love and*

Learning by Jack Canfield, Mark Victor Hansen, and Kimberly Kirberger, or *Chicken Soup for the Soul: The Empowered Woman; 101 Stories about Being Confident, Courageous and Your True Self* by Amy Newmark (and with an awesome story by one of my favorite students, Nancy G. Villalobos).

Jen Sincero has been able to create a specialized offshoot of *You Are a Badass* with her latest title, *You Are a Badass at Making Money: Master the Mindset of Wealth.*

Oprah's *The Wisdom of Sundays* comes with a companion journal called, *The Wisdom Journal: The Companion to the Wisdom of Sundays* by Oprah Winfrey.

Use Your Community

Create a list of your top three to five titles and ask for votes. See which ones get the most hits, which ones seem to roll off the tongue, hook the reader, and create curiosity. A good group of beta title-testers are worth their weight in gold. (If you are still struggling with the title, even after utilizing beta testing, a master brander can be invaluable here.)

Cindy's Title Tale

Let's look at how one author traveled through the title test and how she went from a not-so-hot title to a title she loved.

Cindy had written a book of stories about the resiliency of young women. She had interviewed over one hundred young women who had all faced serious adversity yet were able to push through and find success. She found there was a common thread; the majority of the stories revolved around times when these women had failed, or were challenged, *as the impetus* that pushed them to keep going. Her goal was to change the way young women saw the idea of failure. She hoped that by reading the stories, it might inspire young women to see that failure is not the end of their story; in fact, it may just be the beginning.

Here was Cindy's original title:

The Title Test: *Times We Fail: Stories for and About Young Women*

When I read this title, I thought it was a book about failing. We took the title to a test group and got mixed reactions. Most were confused. Was it a book about failure? Were young women telling stories about other women failing and if so, why? Some stated that it seemed depressing or disheartening. One woman absolutely did not like the word "fail" in the title. Cindy took in all the feedback.

Since Cindy's goal was to inspire and empower, and since many were confused about her core idea, she knew she had not nailed the title. I took her through the title test.

Key #1: Promise

Does the title tell the reader what I am promising, or describe the clear value they will receive if they read my book?

Unfortunately, no, many had no idea how they might benefit from reading the book.

Key #2: Premise

Does the title describe the core concept of the book?

A little; it tells us that there will be stories for and about young women, but it misses the main idea. The main idea is about understanding that the times we fail are actually rocket-booster moments. If we push on, success might just be right around the corner.

Key #3: Approach

Does the title communicate my style?

No. Cindy was energetic and tenacious.

Does the title promote kinship?

A little bit. Again, the subtitle helped: *Stories for and About Young Women* does promote a sense of kinship.

Is the title memorable?

No, not really. Most could not remember the title even a few minutes later.

Is the title relatively short or easy to say?

Yes.

Bonus Question

Does the title communicate dynasty potential and/or journal potential?

People could definitely see a partner journal, especially when they more fully understood the main idea of her book.

Soooo, What Did We Learn?

The test told us that we needed to do more work, that the title was not resonating with readers and, more importantly, it wasn't communicating the core concept. Next, we traveled through the four brainstorming sessions:

Similar-Titles Brainstorm

Cindy went online and looked through several books, downloading many. She found three that she felt had some likeness to hers:

Chocolate for a Teen's Soul: Life-changing Stories for Young Women About Growing Wise and Growing Strong by Kay Allenbaugh

Good Night Stories for Rebel Girls by Elena Favilli and Francesca Cavallo

Women Who Dared: 52 Stories of Fearless Daredevils, Adventurers, and Rebels by Linda Skeers and Livi Gosling

Looking at the words that the authors used, Cindy liked the words "life-changing," "rebel girls," and "dared," though she noticed that most of the books were focusing on successful moments. Her goal was to talk about the moments of failure and inner-grit that ultimately lead to the moment of success. Overall, doing this exercise didn't help with the title, but it made her excited because she found out that there wasn't a book like hers out there.

Personality-of-the-Book Brainstorm

Cindy looked over the personality words. She felt the following words accurately described the personality of her book:

Feisty	Insightful
Educational	Bold
Intellectual	Healing
Calming	Transformative
Thought-provoking	Snarky
Spiritual	Informative
Funny	In-your-face
Fierce	Outrageous

By doing this exercise, Cindy realized that she wanted to communicate a sense of fierce power or boldness.

Feeling-of-the-Book Brainstorm

Cindy looked over the following feeling words. She checked the ones that felt right to her:

Dreamy	Supported
Challenged	Intrigued
Hopeful	Silly
Interested	Provoked
Curious	Enticed
Joyful	Happy
Relaxed	Excited
Smart/educated	Creative
Comforted	Empowered

By doing this exercise, Cindy realized she liked using the word "fail" in her title because she wanted to make people feel curious, challenged, or provoked. Her concept was that she was challenging the very notion that failure was a bad thing or the end of someone's story.

Electric-Words Brainstorm

The last exercise we did was the electric-words brainstorm. This exercise helped shift everything for Cindy.

Cindy's electric words were: fail or failure, stories, resiliency, and young women.

Let's look at her original title once more:

Times We Fail: Stories for and About Young Women

Cindy found it interesting that her original title had "fail," "stories," and "young women."

But she had left out the word "resiliency."

This led her to brainstorm the following two titles:

Times We Fail: Exploring the Nature of Resiliency

The Times We Fail: Stories that Teach Resiliency in Young Women

Cindy really liked the second title. She lived with it for a few weeks. But then, she realized that it was still missing something. The personality of her book was feisty and thought-provoking. She even described the stories to me as fierce, bold, and crackling with energy. I asked if one of these might be another electric word. She smiled.

She finally settled on the title:

The Times We Fail: Stories that Teach Fierce Resiliency in Young Women

Titles and the Three-Key Method: Examples From the Bookshelf

EXAMPLE 1

The Life-Changing Magic of Tidying Up:
The Japanese Art of Decluttering and Organizing
by Marie Kondo

Promise: You can declutter your home and feel much better about your life.

Premise: The KonMari method will teach you a new way to organize all the stuff in your life.

Approach: It will be a no-nonsense, to-the-point read.

Overall assessment of the title: Attention grabbing, memorable, informative but not a synopsis.

EXAMPLE 2

The Gifts of Imperfection:
Let Go of Who You Think You're Supposed to Be
and Embrace Who You Are
by Brené Brown

Promise: You can release perfectionism, shame, and the expectations of others and embrace your unique gifts.

Premise: You will learn the patterns and trends of human behavior from a researcher who will teach you how you may be able to release the patterns that no longer serve you and to embrace more wholehearted living.

Approach: It will be a gentle, hand-holding experience.

Overall assessment of the title: Creates kinship, memorable, informative but not a synopsis.

A Smidge About Covers (and Branding)

But I Want to Do the Cover Myself

Resist this urge at all costs, unless you have been trained. Like, heavily trained. Like, all-of-your-best-friends-are-asking-you-to-do-their-covers-trained.

In this instant-gratification-, short-attention-span-, Twitter-based society, we are lucky if a potential reader has time to even glance at our cover. So, in reality, we may only have seconds to communicate a whole heck of a lot to our reader.

Like It or Not, the Cover Tells the Reader

- if the writer is professional
- if the writer has control of the tone of her book
- how the writer will be communicating her ideas

- the experience they will have while reading the book
- the Three Keys: Promise, Premise, and Approach

Ever had the experience of being inexplicably drawn to a book just by the look of it? You know, when it just feels good to hold it? I recently had this experience when I picked up Natalie MacNeil's book, *The Conquer Kit: A Creative Business Planner for Women Entrepreneurs*. I instantly loved the feel and look of the cover. It felt creative and fun but also incredibly useful. I knew I would buy it within a few seconds of picking it up. Ideally, this is the experience you want your reader to have with your book.

Branding, Branding, Branding

Ah, my friends, this is where I leave you. Any good teacher will tell you what they know and what they don't know. I know a smidge about branding, and I know that all the juicy-good brainstorming we have done will absolutely help you with branding yourself as an author, but I don't even know enough to complete a full paragraph. So, that is why I asked my favorite professional brander for authors, Jeniffer Thompson, to assist. She is going to walk you through the 10 Steps to Personal Branding for the Author (in the bonus chapter, page 301).

Use the blank title test (next page) to test out your potential titles.

The Title Test Worksheet

Key #1: Promise

Does the title tell the reader what I am promising, or describe the clear value they will receive if they read my book? _____

Key #2: Premise

Does the title describe the core concept of the book? _____

Key #3: Approach

Does the title communicate my style? _____

Does the title promote kinship? _____

Is the title memorable? _____

Is the title relatively short or easy to say? _____

Bonus Question

Does the title communicate dynasty potential or journal potential?

_____

Bite-Sized Thoughts for Chapter 15

1. Your title can come to you at any point in the process. Don't worry if it comes to you at the tail end. Just use "working title."

2. There are four brainstorming sessions that can help you unearth your title.

    *   Get to Know the Playing Field = research books that are in some way similar to yours. Pay attention to the words they use in their titles. Which words call to you?
    *   The Personality of the Book = what words would you choose to describe the personality of your book? (Example: informative, funny, spiritual)
    *   The Feeling of the Book = what words would you choose to describe how you want your reader to feel when they pick up your book? (Example: curious, excited, creative)
    *   Electric Words = the words that communicate the essence of your book, they contain a certain kind of authentic energy.

3. Your title should deliver on the Three Keys of Promise, Premise, and Approach. Take your title through the title test to see if it delivers.

    *   Does the title tell the reader what I am promising, or describe the clear value will they receive if they read my book?
    *   Does the title describe the core concept of the book?
    *   Does the title communicate my style?

4. After you brainstorm a few titles, test it out on people who want you to succeed and can be honest and objective.

5. Covers matter. A lot. Don't do the cover yourself. Just please don't.

PART FOUR

GET IT ON THE PAGE

CHAPTER 16

GETTING IT ALL
DOWN ON PAPER

Did I tell you about the time I organized all of my spices alphabetically?

I am trained to maintain focus, get my butt in the chair and put words on the page. Even so, I have found that I can take procrastination to a whole new level. The worst time was when I had a hard deadline for a script and I found myself going into a sort of "procrastination trance." I swear I found everything I could around the house that needed my attention. I found myself inexplicably drawn to old light bulbs, busted screens, and random cat bowls that needed washing. I remember looking around the house and thinking, *I guess that's enough cleaning up, time to write.*

But then I found the spice cabinet. Ah, the spices. Bottles were tilted on their side and old spices had no labels or were seriously expired, not to mention the fact that the food coloring and candy sprinkles had been haphazardly mixed in with the spices. It was pandemonium. How was I ever supposed to cook again if the cinnamon was behind the food coloring and the cardamom label was half torn? I decided right then and there that I absolutely could not write with the spices in such disarray. And, of course, alphabetizing them seemed like the best plan. Many hours later, I woke up from my trance thinking, *does wild thyme go in the W's or the T's?* And the whole day had gone by without a single word on the page.

If you find yourself easily distracted by chaotic spice cabinets, I feel your pain. Here is an organizational tool to help combat any malicious trances that may threaten your consciousness.

Writing Calendars

Are you ready to pour your heart out and get those words on those pages? Are you ready to write this sucker?

(This is where you shout, "YEAH!")

Good. To get yourself organized, it's time to create a writing calendar. This will include a start date and a target finish date. Put some thought into how you will hold yourself accountable and reward yourself. Note that writers track their progress in different ways. As you will see in the sample writing calendar, you can track your progress by counting words or pages completed, or by the number of hours you spent focused on your writing.

The following is a sample writing calendar that will help you to get your first draft done. It includes your writing routine from Chapter 2, thinking through a clear goal, how and when you write best, a weekly check-in with a writing buddy who cares about your progress (I use Sundays but you can pick any day), ideas on how you can be more accountable throughout your months and, lastly, reward stations (what you will give yourself as a reward for tasks completed). Note: If you are working with an agent, manager, or publisher, you may not be able to set your own target date.

No Perfection Required

Don't worry about creating the perfect calendar. Be open to making modifications as you discover what actually works best for you.

_____**'s Writing Calendar**

Target Date for First Draft _____

Start Date _____

Weekly Writing Routine _____

How I Write Best _____

Where I Write Best _____

When I Write Best _____

Sunday Night Check-ins _____

Accountability _____

Rewards Stations _____

WEEK OF	PAGES/WORDS/HOURS	DONE
		☐
		☐
		☐
		☐
		☐
		☐
		☐
		☐
		☐
		☐
		☐
		☐
Completed by:		☐

Examples of Calendars by Real Writers

Mira's Writing Calendar – Three-Month Plan

Start Date: January 20

Target date for first draft: April 22

Word Count Goal: 40,000

Weekly Writing Routine: Mira had a lot of time to dedicate to her book, and her book was a shorter one, approximately 40,000 words. Mira was able to work during the day when her kids were at school. Her goal was to write four days a week, for about four to five hours a day.

Weekly Check-ins: Mira gathered with a few friends and they had an online check-in every Saturday morning (early, around 8 a.m.). They created a Facebook page. Each person posted his or her progress on the morning of the check-in.

Accountability: Mira felt the weekly check-ins with her group would be sufficient accountability.

Rewards Stations: Mira saved money and decided to use it on an upcoming writing conference if she was able to complete her first draft.

Mira's Calendar

WEEK OF	# OF PAGES	DONE
January 8	13	☐
January 15	13	☐
January 22	14	☐
January 29	13	☐
February 5	13	☐
February 12	14	☐
February 19	13	☐
February 26	13	☐
March 5	14	☐
March 12	13	☐
March 19	13	☐
Completed by April 1	14	☐

How It Actually Unfolded for Mira

Start Date: January 2

Actual date first draft completed: May 30 with 39,000 words

Weekly Writing Routine: Mira's mother came to live with them during this time period, and Mira's attention also went to caring for her mom. She was still able to write three days a week, fairly consistently. She also found she had some weeks where she couldn't write at all, where she was pulled in a thousand different directions. Sometimes she would stay up late and when everyone was in bed, she would sneak in a thirty-minute session.

Weekly Check-ins: The Facebook page started out with five members and ended up with three. They did a check-in about every other week, though sometimes they checked in weekly.

Accountability: Mira felt she had enough accountability, but needed a bit more inspiration, so she decided to take a class at the local writing center once a month to keep up her excitement level.

Rewards Stations: Mira was able to go to the writing conference.

Nadia's Writing Calendar – Six-Month Plan

Start Date: January 15

Target Date for First Draft: June 15

Word Count Goal: 50,000

Weekly Writing Routine: Nadia worked full-time and had a family. Her job was flexible, and she could work part-time at home. Her goal was to write three to four afternoons per week.

Sunday Night Check-ins: Nadia selected a friend she was close to in her writing group. They decided to check in with each other every Sunday night.

Accountability: Nadia had a weekly writing group that helped to keep her on track. She also felt that the Sunday night check-ins would help. She had an editor friend that she wanted to read her first draft. She let the editor know when she thought the first draft would be done. Saying it out loud to a professional helped her to feel more accountable.

Rewards Stations: Nadia planned a day out with friends when she completed chapters one through four. She planned a day out alone when she completed chapters five through eight. She planned a day trip with her husband when she finished chapters nine through twelve. Nadia also planned to get a mockup of her cover design created as motivation.

Nadia's Calendar

WEEK OF	# OF WORDS	DONE
January 15	Outline	☐
January 29	Outline	☐
February 5	5,000	☐
February 19	5,000	☐
March 5	5,000	☐
March 19	5,000	☐
April 2	5,000	☐
April 16	5,000	☐
April 30	5,000	☐
May 7	5,000	☐
May 21	5,000	☐
Completed by June 18	5,000	☐

How It Actually Unfolded for Nadia

Start Date: January 15

Actual date first draft completed: August 4 with 48,000 words

Weekly Writing Routine: Nadia was able to work only one to two days per week due to high work demands. She decided she would take a few complete Sundays to do nothing but write. Her family was frustrated, but she promised them that the intense writing period would end.

Sunday Night Check-ins: Nadia tried the check-ins for two months but found it annoying and decided she didn't need them.

Accountability: The weekly writing group helped Nadia to stay on track. She was able to attend approximately two to three meetings a month. Initially, Nadia felt badly that she had shared her target date with her editor friend. But the editor friend assured her it was normal to take longer than expected.

Rewards Stations: Nadia did two out of three of the reward station outings. She said she thought about the reward stations a lot. She wasn't done when she and her husband took their day trip, but the time away gave her perspective. Having a mockup of the cover done was what motivated Nadia the most. She stated that having that cover design made it real for her, which pushed her to complete her first draft.

Elizabeth 's Writing Calendar – One-Year Plan

Start Date: August 1

Target date for first draft: August 15 of the next year

Word Count Goal: 75,000

Weekly Writing Routine: Elizabeth worked full-time and had two kids. With the support of her husband, she decided her writing routine would be to get up sixty to ninety minutes early and do a session every day.

Weekly Check-ins: Sarah hired a writing coach. The goal was to meet on her lunch hour every other week. She would email her progress weekly (on Sunday nights) to her writing coach.

Accountability: Besides hiring a writing coach, Elizabeth told her husband, who she felt could be "naggy," that she needed his help with accountability. She thought his somewhat pushy personality would be a good thing for this particular goal.

Rewards Stations: Elizabeth loved shoes. For each month that she completed her writing goal, she celebrated with a new pair of shoes.

Elizabeth's Calendar

WEEK OF	# OF HOURS	DONE
August 5	6	☐
August 12	6	☐
August 19	10	☐
August 26	6	☐
September 2	6	☐
September 9	12	☐
September 16	6	☐
September 23	6	☐
September 30	10	☐
October 7	6	☐
October 14	6	☐
(This went on for fifty-two weeks, using a similar pattern.)		
Completed by August 15		☐

How It Actually Unfolded for Elizabeth

Start Date: *August 8*

Actual date first draft completed: *October 1 with 81,000 words*

Weekly Writing Routine: *Elizabeth started out getting up every day to write for an hour. She was able to write about three times a week and would grab a few hours on a Saturday or Sunday when she could.*

Weekly Check-ins: *Elizabeth was able to have weekly contact with her writing coach, sometimes by Skype if Elizabeth was out of town on business. On average, she met with her writing coach about three times a month.*

Accountability: *Her husband's check-ins worked for about three months. Then she decided that he was just making her nuts, and she moved to just working with her writing coach for accountability.*

Rewards Stations: *Elizabeth had a lot of shoes by the end of the whole experience.*

Note: In all the above examples, it took the writer longer to finish than their initial target date. Though it's common to take longer than you expect, it doesn't always work out that way. In fact, some finish before their target date. However, all the three writers above shared that having a target end-date pushed them to go faster than they would have gone without creating a target date.

Q: What Happens If I Don't Hit Each Mark on Time?

A: You can alter your worksheet as you go. Don't be hard on yourself; **movement is movement and every bit counts**. Changing up how you get it all done is perfectly normal. Be open to modifications. Find what works and do more of it. If something doesn't work, ditch it.

I once had a client tell me, "I keep having to put my book on the back burner." Her family needed her, she was needed at work, and the book never seemed to get the attention it deserved. She wondered if she should just let it go—thinking she would never get the draft done. I told her that low and slow still gets the stew cooked, and sometimes it tastes even better with all that marinating. When she handed me her finished draft she said, "It's true; I thought it would never happen, but even things on the back burner eventually get cooked!"

Q: What Happens If I Get Stuck and Don't Know What to Write?

A: If you find yourself freezing when you look at the blank page, remember you can either

- Sequence it (using your outline, write one chapter, then the next, then the next).

Or:

- Frankenstein it (using your outline, write the pieces that are calling to you, the ones you want to write when you want to write them, knowing that eventually all the pieces will be written.

Your goal here is to complete a crappy first draft. That's right. No first draft is beautiful. First drafts are meant to be clunky and uneven with bits of delicious writing gold. Having realistic expectations can be a game changer for new writers.

Getting It Done Using the Let-It-Go Method

"I stare at the screen and cry." This is what one writer told me when I asked her how she came up with answers to the problematic areas in her book.

"Does it work?" I asked.

She thought. She paced. She nodded. "Eventually."

I asked her to watch her own behavior for a week and to decide how and when the answers came to her. I asked her to pay attention to what she was doing, where she was and the time of day. As a therapist, I had been trained in solution-focused therapy, so I was looking for a pattern. The bottom line is this → If it doesn't work, stop doing it. Once you find something that does work, even a little bit, do more of it.

Here's what she discovered. The answers came to her *when she wasn't staring at the screen.* The answers came to her when she was taking a shower, walking the dog, driving, or cooking.

She was not alone. Most writers reported that their best ideas or solutions to their biggest problems came to them when they had temporarily put the writing aside.

The 4-Step Let-It-Go Method

1. Ask yourself a specific question. (Examples: *What should the title of the book be?* or *How should I end this chapter?* or *Which story should I choose?*)
2. Put the question in your "subconscious think tank" and **let it go.**
3. Have no specific time limit.
4. At your most relaxed, ask your subconscious for some answers. Then when ready, do a pouring session. Just place

pen to paper and allow anything and everything to pour out of you.

Other Problem-Solving Ideas When You Feel Stuck or All Tapped out

- Take a walk; get out into nature.
- Brainstorming sessions: try not thinking so much and just return to free-form pouring sessions.
- Write down ten ideas (one will most likely be good).
- Phone a friend: call a writing buddy.
- Do a meditative task slower than usual, like cooking, gardening, or going for a walk.
- Ask a professional: ask your writing teacher, editor, or writing coach for ideas.
- Work to prompts: Go online and write down some writing prompts or use a cool book like Judy Reeves's *A Writer's Book of Days.*

What to Do When Your First Draft Is Done

Once your first draft is done, take a break. Seriously. Take at least two to four weeks off (but not much longer because you want to stay engaged with the process). Then sit down and read your book from the point of view of your target audience. Put on your first-time-reader hat. Just do the best you can. You may find that you are too close to the material and can't read it objectively. No problem. That's what writing coaches, beta readers, and editors are for. A fresh pair of eyes can be invaluable.

Q: What Is a Beta Reader?

A: A beta reader is a reader who would normally be in your target audience, who reads the book at an early stage, and offers constructive feedback. This is important: well-meaning friends and family are generally not the best beta readers (though there are exceptions). I can't exactly tell you why, but in my experience, most writers find themselves feeling discouraged after close friends and family read their first draft. The relationship you have with the person tends to color how they feel about the book. You want a pair of eyes that will evaluate the work *and only the work.*

Q: How Do I Find a Beta Reader?

A: Other writers often make great beta readers. Join writing organizations or get yourself into a writing group. Or, if you would like some professional feedback, getting input from a professional developmental editor can be of tremendous help. The professional will know what to look for, they will know what you are doing right, and will, hopefully, know how to encourage you to do more of that. A qualified professional can also make fast and clear recommendations on how and where to cut.

Q: What Is the Most Common Problematic Issue for First-Time Writers?

A: By far, the most common issue is that new writers want to be done after their first draft. Yet that rarely, if ever, happens. This is what I often see happening:

You type the last sentence.

The first draft is done! Yahoo! You celebrate. Major accomplishment.

Nervously and cautiously, you hand it over to a professional writing coach or editor (remember moms and best friends don't count).

Feelin' the Blues – Part One:

You may experience some postpartum first-draft blues or some separation anxiety here. Prepare yourself. It's can be a strange feeling or possibly anti-climactic to hand over your first draft. Do some extra self-care during this time period.

The professional reads the first draft and offers feedback, basically saying something like, "Good job, but...."

In other words, there is a lot of great stuff in that first draft, but it will need to be rewritten.

Feelin' the Blues – Part Two:

You despair. Life is over. How could all of your dreams and hopes be dashed? You think, I will never be able to do it right. You wonder, maybe I should just quit.

Then you wait a few days, and reread the notes. You let it all sink in. If you have a good editor or writing coach, they will have given you clear insights and steps to take to improve your book.

Common First-draft Notes Include

- reorganizing the material so that it has a smoother flow
- the writer needs to add in more of her voice
- a lot needs to be cut due to repetition
- part of the book is unclear and needs to be clarified

And here is the weird (and unexpected part). The writer usually takes some time to think, percolate, toss and turn it all over in her mind, and then they come up with an answer to the big issues **in a way that feels right for them**. Often it is something unforeseen by the editor, but it answers the major problematic issues.

I have noticed that if a writer can get over the first-draft-notes blues, and come back to make the second draft their own, they will survive the rest of the process. Somehow the shock of going from draft one to draft two is the biggest obstacle. Draft three and four seem to be less scary and intimidating. Sometimes it's because the writer has moved into polishing and has all their major ideas more or less down and in place. Sometimes it's because they better understand the process of receiving notes and making changes to make the work stronger. Confidence grows with each draft.

Don't Forget to

- Listen to the soul of the book when it starts talking to you.
- Gather your team of professionals to help you with the next steps (content editing, copy editing).
- Get used to discomfort. Discomfort means you are growing.
- Applaud the small moments of growth. Don't let them pass you by. The process itself and all the milestones along the way are worth celebrating.

Bite-Sized Thoughts for Chapter 16

1. To get yourself organized, you will need to think through your tenacious writing routine and create a writing calendar. Your writing calendar will include a start date and a target finish date, and how you will hold yourself accountable and reward yourself.

2. Don't worry about creating the perfect calendar. Just give your best guess. Then be open to making modifications as you discover what works best for you.

3. To keep the flow of fresh ideas coming, take walks, get out into nature, and use the Let-It-Go method.

4. It's normal and natural for the process to take longer than you expect. Do not beat yourself up. Writing is not linear and can be an extraordinarily messy process. Just keep moving.

5. Even the pots on the back burner eventually cook.

CHAPTER 17

FAQS – TROUBLESHOOTING

I wish I could sit with each and every one of you and walk you through your questions. But I will offer you the next best thing. These are the most common questions I receive as a writing coach—so, if you are struggling, hopefully you will find an answer here.

Q: What If I Realize I Need to Do More Research?

A: This is normal and, to some degree, expected. Don't fret. It's common when writing your book to realize areas that you have holes that feel incomplete or unfinished. Writing is sometimes a process of learning what you don't know. Take a breath, roll up your sleeves, and go have some fun discovering new information.

Q: What If I Get Frustrated With the Writing Process and Want to Give Up?

A: All I can say is, being a marriage and family therapist has come in handy as a writing coach. One reason is that sometimes writers come to me when they are ready to divorce their books. **Don't do it.** Give it time. Remember when you were newly in love? Give it a bit of separation time (not too much, though) and then do your best to bring yourself back to your initial spark of interest. Remember why you wanted to write your book in the first place. Once you reconnect to your initial passion, it will carry you through. Also, a strong weekly writing group can be invaluable to help you sustain motivation.

Q: How Do I Decide Which Optional Elements to Include in My Template?

A: By looking over the templates, you already know if you gravitate more toward a discussion of big ideas, or using stories as a way of covering your big ideas, or if you have an actionable plan that you want to convey. Now you may be wondering which optional elements to put into place. My advice is to ask:

Does it pass the Helpful, Essential test?

Only include what you feel is necessary and authentic. We don't have the attention span for the filler. Readers notoriously skip prefaces, forewords, and introductions. That's not to say that you shouldn't include them. But only include what you feel is essential.

As an example, if you have received a lot of praise for your book, then you will want to have a "Praise For" section. If you want to acknowledge people for their part in your career, then you will want to have an acknowledgment section. If you have taught your theory to many groups and you know the common places that readers can get confused, then a "how to read this book" section will be essential. If you have a highly respected person in the field that supports your book, then you will want to have a foreword. If you have a quote that encapsulates your entire theory into a wonderfully concise saying, then yes, use a quote at the beginning of your book.

Q: What If I Choose a Template, Create an Outline but Then Realize It Needs to Be Changed Later?

A: Absolutely nothing is set in stone until the end. It's totally normal to course correct. It's one thing to have a theoretical map before you set out to sea. It's another thing to be at sea. Be flexible.

Q: Can I Mix and Match Parts of the Templates?

A: Yes! Your template should reflect who you are and how you communicate. Just pay attention to the Helpful, Essential test. For example, you can add stories into the Big Ideas Template or the Plan-of-Action Template. You may have a chapter that outlines the theory and then back it up with a short anecdote. Or you may describe an actionable plan, then offer a story that illustrates how that actionable item can be played out in the real world.

Remember that there is no need to reinvent the wheel here. Look at the books you admire. Get a sense for how they are organized. Look at the length. Look at the book size. See how many chapters there are. Do they use stories, facts, research, or quotes? Do they break their book into sections or parts? How do they entice you to read more in the first chapter or make you want to follow through in the last chapter?

Q: What If My Perfectionism Gets in the Way of Me Completing My Book?

A: The best way I can answer this question is to tell you that I still feel the book you are holding in your hands is incomplete. I have worked on it for years and have put in hundreds of hours of research, writing, and rewriting. I have gone through three rounds of beta readers and three editors. My point is, even if I worked on this book for another five years, I bet I would still feel a sense of it being incomplete. Most writers feel this way. The sense that there is a perfect "done" moment is a myth. If you are a perfectionist, you will have to allow your book to leave your hands and make its way into the world with a little itching sensation like you could have done more. Know that there are always more books to write. And, as one of my favorite thought leader authors, Nicole Weiss, says, perfect is the enemy of done.

Q: It Seems Like There Are a Bunch of Kinds of Editors; Can You Explain What Each One of Them Does?

A: Most people will agree that there are three types of book editors. (Some may overlap in what they do.)

Each editor is needed during different parts of the writing journey. The first type is the developmental editor, who looks at the big picture and the general substance. The second type is the copy or line editor, that looks at the nitty gritty before you submitty. The third is the proofreader, or the last point of contact before your work is born into the world (checks the copy in its entirety to make sure it is ready for publication). Let's dive a little deeper into each one.

Editor #1: Developmental or Content Editor—The "BIG PICTURE" Editor (Sometimes Known As a Writing Coach)

Full disclosure: This is the kind of editing I do, and I know it most intimately.

A developmental or content editor looks at the big picture. Many writers choose to work with a developmental editor before they begin the writing process (by that I mean the-words-on-the-page stage) to hone the idea and help craft the outline, uncover their writing voice, brainstorm tone, and choose a template. This type of editor sits down with you and looks at your idea, your dreams and goals, and helps you to make a plan to execute your vision.

You may also seek out a developmental editor after you have completed a draft and before you start the query process, or if you have submitted and are not receiving the kind of response that you had hoped for. If you are receiving comments like "uneven" or "good idea but not well executed" or some version of "almost," a developmental editor can be an invaluable asset to keep your work from ending up in the slush pile.

The developmental editor can assist you in creating and developing any or all of the following: your core idea, structure and template, tone, writer's voice, and general marketability of concept. In other words, they can help you develop the full plan (or story, or world) that you will use to write your book.

Once you have a first draft (or even a chunk of pages), a developmental editor can offer analysis and specific suggestions about the concept, structure, organization, style, flow, tone, and presentation.

For Nonfiction, Content Editors Look at

- Structure
- Organization of ideas
- Voice
- Theme
- Style of writing
- Pacing
- Tone
- Description and detail
- Thoroughness of the argument
- Effectiveness of the argument
- Approach to the thesis or core idea
- Marketability
- Target audience (Are you giving them what you promised and what they need?)

Once the BIG PICTURE issues are solved, most of the time you can stay with your developmental editor and zoom in a bit on the material to check it out for style and flow.

With All of the Above in Mind, They Look at the Material and Address Questions Like

- Is this material clear and understandable?
- Does the information have a smooth and easy flow?

- Does one idea support the next?
- Is the information presented accurately?

To improve the flow of the piece, the editor may write or rewrite sections, reorganize paragraphs, suggest changes to the order of chapters, and assist with introductions and conclusions of your material. They may also make suggestions as to places you can cut, trim or revise in order to improve the overall readability and clarity.

Some developmental editors get in there and assist with research, offer resources, and help with the rewriting process.

Marni says: While most developmental editors assist with style and flow, some stop after the big picture and refer you to the copy or line editor for the paragraph and sentence structure issues.

Editor #2: The Copy Editor (or Line) Editor—or What I Call: "The Nitty Gritty Before I Submitty" Editor

When most writers think of an editor, they think of this person. The copy or line editor dives in and makes sure the document is in order so that it can be presented professionally. This is the last stop before submitting to an agent or publisher.

Copy editors will check and correct most or all of these aspects: spelling, punctuation, grammar, syntax, word usage (or over usage), consistency of style, and format.

Some copy editors will read the draft as if they are a beta reader and offer notes or changes that will enhance overall clarity and flow.

A good copy/line editor will always try to respect the author's voice and try to fulfill the author's original meaning. In other words, your book should still say what you want to say, and it should still sound like you.

They may cross check your references, facts and figures, tables, quotes, infographics, and illustrations to make sure that the information in the text is consistent and accurate. If they find copyrighted material, they may alert you to the need to gain permission for use. When completed, most copy editors will provide a manuscript with track changes engaged so that the author or publisher can accept or reject each edit. Often times, the author or publisher returns it for a final/cleanup edit.

Editor #3: The Proofreader—or the "Are We Good to Go?" Editor

A proofreader looks at the formatted manuscript and makes the final assessment on how it looks. They look for any leftover errors or inconsistencies that the author or the previous editor(s) may have made (it's hard to catch everything). They notice any typographical errors or any errors in typesetting. This editor looks at the last version that the copy editor and writer signed off on and they ask, *are there any discrepancies? Did the typesetter make any errors? How does the page look? Is the layout correct?*

In my experience, some copy editors also offer proofing services.

Q: So, When Do I Employ the Different Kinds of Editors?

A: First, figure out where you are in the writing process.

Prewriting

If you are just starting out in the process and want some help developing your core idea, a developmental editor or a writing coach is a great place to start.

If you have a first draft and you are not sure what you have exactly, you may want an assessment or critique from a developmental editor.

With prewriting, you do not need the other types of editors.

After Fifty (or so) Pages or After the First Draft

At this stage, you can still work with a developmental editor. Since they do both assessments and reworking of the material itself, you want to figure out what you need. Ask:

Do I want a critique? (Where someone tells me what is working and what is not working and how to fix it.)

Or:

Do I want someone just to get in there and fix what is not working?

Marni says: My advice is to get a critique first, as it is less expensive and you may be able to make many of the changes yourself. You can always move on to the "just fix it" phase where you have an editor smooth it out and make it all pretty.

Once you are clear on what you want, ask your editor if they perform that service. If not, ask for referrals. (A good editor will have referrals.)

Q: Once I Find an Editor That I Want to Work With, How Do I Approach Them?

A: Interview them respectfully. Ask the editor what types of editing they do and be specific about it. (Don't be afraid to ask questions; if they can't take questions, they are not the right editor for you.)

Questions to Ask

- What type of editing do you do?
- How do you define the type of editing? As I mentioned, some editors use different language—so it

is entirely appropriate to ask for clarification as to what services they are offering.

- How do you charge? (For example: by the hour, word, or project.)
- What will I receive as feedback?
- How specific will your notes be? How do you provide the notes? (For example: on the text itself, in a separate document.)
- How long will it take?
- Do you have any testimonials or former clients I can speak to? (If this editor is a referral, you can skip this step.)
- Can I speak with you if I have follow-up questions?
- How would you like to receive my material?

Marni says: Editors may have their own best practices for submissions. However, here are some general guidelines. Submit in a Word doc or rich text file. Your page size should be 8.5 by 11; your paragraphs should be double spaced and 12-point font. Place one-inch margins on the top and bottom.

Remember that your editor does not need to be your best friend. One of my most talented editors told me, "I'm not your best friend; I'm the best friend of the material." You want your editor to tell you the truth. Still, it's important to know if you tend to be delicate with feedback. If so, you may want an editor with a gentler touch so that you will stay in the process.

Overall: Don't be afraid to ask questions. If this is your first experience with an editor, give yourself time to become acquainted with the process and be patient as you stumble through it. No matter which kind of editor you hire, make sure you both understand what work will be included, and get that understanding in writing, either in a contract or in emails. Try to go with referrals from a trusted source. The best editors are known within their writing communities.

Q: How Do I Sell My Book Once It's Done?

A: As we talked about in Chapter 4, many authors act more like entrepreneurs, taking over platform building, marketing, and PR. A few helpful books to get you started down this road are

- *APE: Author, Publisher, Entrepreneur—How to Publish a Book* by Guy Kawasaki and Shawn Welch
- *Create Your Writer Platform: The Key to Building an Audience, Selling More Books, and Finding Success as an Author* by Chuck Sambuchino
- *Guerrilla Marketing for Writers: 100 No-Cost, Low Cost Weapons for Selling Your Work* by Jay Conrad Levinson, Rick Frishman, Michael Larsen, and David L. Hancock

Q: Marni, What If I Am Just Too Overwhelmed and Don't Want Anything to Do With the Marketing and PR Aspects of My Book?

A: Well, if you don't mind paying for the services, there is a person (or a team) that will happily take over all of that for you. But first, we should define what "PR" and "marketing" mean. It can be downright confusing because the job descriptions often sound similar, the two services can overlap, and social media has caused the lines to blur. Having said that, in a traditional sense, here is the breakdown.

Public Relations: This person will assist with the overall promotion and maintenance of creating a favorable public image for you as an author, coach, or service provider. (Think: image, reputation, how people view you. If you get noticed in the press, receive an award, get some buzz from industry influencers, or a slew of social media followers, the PR campaign was successful.)

Marketing: By doing market research and creating advertising, this person will aid you in actively promoting and selling your books, services, or products. (Think: promoting and selling your books. If you sold a good number of books, services, or products, then the marketing campaign was successful.)

Tips on hiring someone for PR/Marketing: Use professionals that are knowledgeable or heavily weighted toward authors and books. If they tend to sell widgets, they won't know the book-promotion-and-selling business. Get a referral if possible—this is where networking with a writing association (see Appendix 1 on page 317 for a few options) can help. If you can't get a referral, make sure the professionals have been around awhile. Ask lots of questions. I love the question, "If my campaign is a success, what will we have achieved?"

Q: If I Want to Go the Traditional Route, Do You Have Any Suggestions for Further Reading?

A: There is so much free, valuable content online on the subject, that it never hurts to start there. As far as books go, I love Jane Friedman (even though she spells her name wrong). Her book, *The Business of Being a Writer (Chicago Guides to Writing, Editing, and Publishing)* covers more than just traditional publishing, it's a comprehensive writing information feast. Another reliable pal is *The Writers Market: The Most Trusted Guide to Getting Published* edited by Robert Lee Brewer (grab the most recent year).

Q: What Are Some Common First-Timer Writer Mistakes?

A: If you struggle with self-esteem → apologizing for or equivocating about your knowledge. (Saying things like, "It may just be me but…" or "you may think differently but…."

If you are an academic or a lawyer → your language may come out too stilted or stiff.

If you are a therapist → your language may come out a bit too clinical.

If you are a journalist → you may leave yourself out of your writing.

If you are a quote lover → you may overuse quotes. (I don't know why we do this.)

So, what to do?

For the first draft, just get the words down on the page. Then, you can adjust accordingly. It's not at all uncommon that a writer's second draft is about adjusting the language until you get the exact tone that you want.

CHAPTER 18

WHAT NEXT?

Sisters, your ideas matter. Your experience matters. Your expertise matters. The world is waiting for your voice.

—Vanessa Wakeman, thought leadership expert

be the smoke signal
be the horn
or be the water
but just be

I was walking in the desert. It had been a year since my father passed rather suddenly, and I was looking for some solace when the words above came to me. I had also reached the end of the writing of this book and I wasn't sure how to close it out. I sat on a rock; I didn't fully understand the message. *What did it mean?*

I sat and waited. And heard more.

The writer who uses smoke signals speaks from a spiritual place, with intent to reach the heavens. The writer who uses the horn speaks from a place of confidence, with intent to be a part of the music of life. The writer who uses the water speaks from a place of gentle conviction, slowly, and forever, changing the shape of the conversation.

I don't like the endings. I don't like to say goodbye. It's like we've spent all this time together and then, so long? So, I will end with this. I hope one day we meet. I hope you will believe in the part of you that wants to roar. I hope you will recognize yourself as the smoke signal, the horn, or the water. I hope that whatever form you choose, you jump into this journey with a full heart. This is a dynamic time we are living in. And we need your book to help shape these times. We need your voice. We need you.

—Marni Rachel Freedman

Okay, now go. Write. Roar.

Now.

JOIN THE COMMUNITY

Ways to Connect with Marni

Go to
MarniFreedman.com
to sign up for the
Thought Leaders Who Write Newsletter

Get your FREE workbook:
21 Days to Boost Your Writing Confidence.

Facebook
facebook.com/MarniFreedmanWritersCoach

Twitter
@Marnifreedy

ABOUT THE AUTHOR

Marni Freedman (BFA, LMFT) is a produced, published, and award-winning writer. After graduating as an award-winning student from the USC School of Filmic Writing, Marni began her career with her play *Two Goldsteins on Acid*, which was produced in Los Angeles. She worked as a script doctor for top film companies and worked as a script agent for the Mary Sue Seymour Agency. One of her plays was made into a film, *Playing Mona Lisa*, and was produced by Disney. Her most recent play, *A Jewish Joke*, co-written with Phil Johnson, ran in San Diego and was critically acclaimed. It is currently touring the country and will soon be making its off-Broadway debut. Marni teaches at UCSD Extension, San Diego Writers, Ink, and The Center for Creative Aging. She runs the successful San Diego Writers Network and produces a yearly theatrical Memoir Showcase. Marni edits the anthologies *The Literary Vine* (published by Wolfheart Press) and *Shaking the Tree: brazen. short. memoir.* (published by MCM Publishing).

Marni is also a therapist for artists and writers. Her welcoming, easygoing nature and solid background are the underpinnings of what makes her such a popular writing coach across the country. Marni is a unique writing coach because she has a tool for almost everything. She has a way of taking complicated information and translating it into easy-to-grasp, step-by-step information. Her character worksheets and plotting devices have been met with rave reviews. Marni's next two books, *The Memoir Map* and *Writing to Heal,* will be released in December of 2019. You can also find Marni at thefeistywriter.com, a writing hub to help writers find and believe in their authentic voice.

ALSO BY MARNI FREEDMAN

Marni's first book on writing, *7 Essential Writing Tools: That Will Absolutely Make Your Writing Better (And Enliven Your Soul)* is an international bestseller. Marni invites you to fall in love with the magic that is writing with writer-tested-and-approved tools on story structure, scene creation, plot, voice, and character.

The Master Coach Offers Fresh and Practical Ideas on Writing, Including

- The 15 Essential Plot Spots—a plotting tool for everything from novels to memoirs to screenplays
- The Big List of 55 Character Archetypes
- Insights into Figuring out How You (Yes, You) Work as a Writer

- The 5 Elements That Will Ensure You Have a Compelling Story Idea
- A Clear Explanation of Anti-heroes, Anti-villains, and Everything In-between
- The 9 Elements of Crafting a Dynamic Character
- 3 Steps to Finding and Boldly Using Your Unique Writer's Voice

You need this kind of kick in the pants.

CHAPTER 19

BONUS CHAPTER: WHAT'S BRANDING GOT TO DO WITH IT?

By Jeniffer Thompson

Ten Steps to Personal Branding for the Author

What's Branding Got to Do with It?

> *Everyone has talent. What is rare is the courage to follow the talent to the dark place where it leads.*
>
> —Erica Jong, *Fear of Flying*

Personal branding is not a revolutionary concept, but it's relatively new to authors. A personal brand can help to establish your authority, catapult your success, and solidify your future. Here's a little secret: Most entrepreneurs and authors promote their books and services, but they fail to promote themselves. Create a strong personal brand and one-time customers become loyal followers, and dare I say, fans. By branding you, you create fans.

Consider your favorite brands for a moment, brands like Nike, Coca Cola, and Starbucks. The brand is not only the product—it's the experience. More importantly, it's the promise. We trust these brands because we know what to expect.

Starbucks, for example, sells coffee. Pretty expensive coffee for that matter, and yet their success allows them to open stores across the street from other Starbucks. Their brand offers the promise of convenience, as well as ambiance and a specific flavor of coffee-drink. You've come to expect a Starbucks on every corner, with free Wi-Fi and a comfortable place to sit and work. It's not really about the coffee. Starbucks makes good on their promise and we appreciate that promise. Why? Because we know what to expect and we trust it.

What's your personal promise? How do you want people to describe you? What do you want to be known for? What experience or feeling do you want your readers to have when they read your books? What do you want them to do? Answering these questions before you begin your brand development will help you ensure that the language of your brand reflects your true passion and your goals, while also reaching your ideal reader.

What's Revolutionary?

As a writer, the fact that you can deliver your message to the people who need it most, and you *can* do it from the comfort of your own home (or Starbucks) is not just critical, it's revolutionary, and it's leveling the playing field. What I'm talking about is how the internet has changed the way we communicate. Getting the word out is no longer about how much money you have to spend on radio adverts and billboard signs; it's about how well you know your audience and then consistently offering them valuable content. If your message is packaged in a professional way, even better; your audience is more likely to recognize your brand and trust it. Then, not only do they remember you, but they tell others about you—they become invested in you.

Authors often ask me how to sell more. The answer?

- Know your audience,
- connect with them in a meaningful and memorable way, then
- stay connected.

And in today's marketplace, all of that is within your control. Defining your personal style so that you resonate with your audience and developing your online presence so that others sit up and take notice are now highly doable.

Let Your "Roaring Voice" Push You Out of Your Comfort Zone

When I think of all the women who have accomplished great things and who've had the most impact on our world, I think of the attribute they must all have in common: courage. Marni tapped into this earlier in the book when she discussed finding the part of you that is ready to roar. I want you to continue working with that part of yourself to uncover and shape your personal brand.

It takes a hell of a lot of courage to believe in yourself, to step out of your comfort zone and disrupt the norm. It takes courage to shout your truth to the world and *trust* that what you have to say is not only worthy, but important, critical even.

Dream Bigger Than You Did Yesterday

Throw out any self-doubt or negative talk that tells you that you don't need a brand, or that you can't do it, and then, dream big! Even if you think, "Oh, I could never do that," dream it anyway. Give yourself permission to be creative and ask for what you want—if you have the courage to dream it, you are that much closer to making it happen.

The number-one thing I hear from my branding clients is, "Who am I to have a brand? What makes me special?"

Here's the deal. You are special. You have a superpower, a gift that makes you singular and unique. The key is to identify your superpower and then have the courage to build upon it and shout your message to the world.

Do you want to be famous, make a difference, make money? You gotta be honest with yourself. It takes courage to say, "Yes, I want to be famous!" Know your truth before you begin the journey.

Are you willing to put in the work? It takes time, commitment, sacrifice, and a lot of courage to make it big. You have to be willing to fail, and willing to begin again, and again. Be realistic. Simply throwing money at a situation won't make it work. It might help short-term, but winning at the long game of success requires the kind of passion and drive where you never take no for an answer. Not from you, not from anyone.

It takes courage to get out of bed every day and believe that you are worthy, capable, and unique.

Are You Ready? The Ten Steps to Personal Branding

Even if you have doubt, that's okay, you can still take steps and begin the journey toward your goal. Trust that you will build confidence and courage along the way. It's the "doing" part that counts, ignoring the fear and doing it anyway. Self-doubt is common and perhaps even necessary; it helps us stay on top of our game, to try harder, to always learn and improve. Just don't let it stop you from moving forward.

Having a brand can provide you with a roadmap that keeps you going, even when you feel like your self-confidence is waning. I have noticed time and time again that the momentum of your brand will keep rolling and will begin to take on a life of its own.

A personal brand gives you the ability to continually build upon even the smallest of achievements, to capitalize upon on all of your successes, to stay relevant, and to continually strive to improve, to be better—to be great.

1. Imagine Your Success Line to Help Illuminate Your Goals

I'd like you to take a moment and imagine your success line, that is, the line that begins right here, right now, and runs into the place in time where you have achieved success.

What does your success look like? Where do you live? How are you making an impact? What do you look like? More importantly, how does the world view this successful you? Are you famous? What do you get up in the morning and dedicate your life to accomplishing? How do you feel?

Once you have a clear picture of what success looks and feels like, I want you to work backward along your success line and visualize the milestones that you will need to meet to achieve that success. What items might be on your roadmap? Things like publishing your book, speaking at industry conferences, contributing articles to well-known magazines in your field, giving a TED Talk, appearing on well-known podcasts, building a mailing list of fans ... your roadmap items will be unique to you. These are your tangible goals, and even if they seem lofty, I encourage you to let them take shape. This is the making of your roadmap, your success plan, and it's all moving toward creating your personal brand.

2. Discover What You Are Willing to Invest, and Create a Budget

Your budget is not just about money; it's about time, and even more importantly, it's about your emotional bandwidth.

When it Comes to Money

How much money can you comfortably invest? Get acquainted with both the low-budget and the higher-budget investments. Once you have a dollar amount in mind, you can budget for the things that will help build your brand in stages. You don't have to do it all right now, but you need a plan to get it all done at a comfortable pace.

When it Comes to Time and Emotional Bandwidth

How much time do you have to invest? How much bandwidth? Ask yourself how you want to spend your time. How comfortable are you with performing, or learning about the various tools available to you: blogging, social networking, podcasting, writing, video, speaking? In other words, uncover what gets you excited and brings you joy.

Contrary to popular opinion, you do not need to do it all. In fact, if you choose to employ methods that exhaust you, then those methods, and the time you spend doing them, will ensure that you never reach your end-goal because you'll end up broke, fatigued, and burned out.

Know all aspects of your budget, and stick to what is comfortable—remember, this is a long-term plan. It won't happen overnight.

3. Claim Your Unique Voice

Please don't worry about whether or not there are other people out there doing what you do. Demand for your type of ability is a good thing. It tells you that there's an audience for your message. And no matter how many of "them" there are out there, there is only one you.

Here's the key: what about your message is unique? Maybe you're funny, or lyrical, or well-researched.

If this is hard for you

- I encourage you to sit down with friends or colleagues. Ask them to describe who you are at work. Ask them what they consider your superpower to be. Ask them what you are good at, and conversely what you're not so good at. This exercise may require some serious self-analysis. It requires you to be open and honest with yourself and capable of hearing constructive feedback.

- I encourage you to develop a list of core values. Core values are the fundamental beliefs that drive your actions and decisions. These are the basis for what will make you unique and help you remain consistent and true to your brand. For larger companies, core values are handed down among the ranks as a barometer for how to act and how to treat others, used as a guide to ensure that the company is on track. For you, it's a reminder of why you do what you do and how you do it.

4. Know Your Audience on an Intimate Level

Your brand is ultimately your promise to your target audience.

Where is your audience? What social platforms do they hang out on? What magazines do they read? Where do they get their news? Knowing your target audience means understanding their needs and desires. Identify what your audience needs and how you can serve them. If you know what they need right now, you can provide value for the long-term.

Marni asked you to think about this a bit when she talked about knowing the needs of your readers. Defining your audience is key. Guess what is the most common answer to the question, who is your audience? Unfortunately, the usual response is, "Everyone is my audience."

"Everyone" is a tough target to hit. And if you try to reach everyone, you'll reach no one. This isn't as much about demographics as it is about targeting the person you'll enjoy working with the most. I recommend that you identify a persona, or avatar, to serve as your ideal client. Give this person a name and a history and then think about how you can serve this one person.

5. Know Who Influences Your Audience

I'm talking about your competition and the people who influence your buyers—these are the people who currently live and work in the space where your audience exists. They are fellow writers, authors, speakers, and thought leaders. These are the people you will learn the most from, the people you need to get close to. Ultimately, you only need to identify one influencer to find them all.

The internet is a glorious place for research. If you're not comfortable using search engines like Google, then you need to change that. And the only way to better navigate Google is to start navigating Google. Start by searching the name of one influencer. Google will then give you recommendations on the right side of your search results screen; it's called, "People also search for…." which is followed by a list of possible influencers you can research.

Pay attention to how you search and which searches are most effective. Note the places where your influencer appears online, where she writes, the comments on her articles, what social platforms she's active on (and which ones get the most engagement), who follows her and engages with her content, where she speaks (and the other speakers and influencers who speak there), how her bio reads, who she follows (because you will follow them too)—note it all; this is a great way to fill in those milestones for your roadmap.

Follow your influencers on social media and subscribe to their newsletters. Comment on and share their posts. Also, pay attention to ways in which you can help this person. What is missing from her narrative that you can add to? Do you see possible partnerships or collaboration opportunities? And lastly, what is she doing that you can do better?

Set a plan in place to get close to your influencers and become known to them.

6. Research and Collect Data

As you research, be sure to track it all—do not do this later. Create a tracking system that works for you (spreadsheets, Google Drive, a physical notebook that you carry with you, an app on your phone, etc.).

Every time you are inspired by a conversation, a podcast, or an article, or you just randomly have a good idea—write it down. And here's the key: check in on your ideas once a week and create a system for putting these good ideas to work. Every "aha" moment is another building block in the foundation of your success.

7. Create Your Personal Roadmap

Remember your success line? Now it's time to build the roadmap that will guide you to the end of the line. Create a plan to meet those milestones and schedule them out for the next year. Things like content creation, networking, article submissions, speaking, and social media. Remember your budget. Don't overcommit, or your plan will not be sustainable.

Even just a rough idea of where you are going helps you get there eventually, but a solid plan (a roadmap) ensures that you not only get there, but that you get there on time and on budget. Plus, a solid roadmap ensures that nothing slips through the cracks.

Go back to your success line and visualize each goal in your mind's eye, asking, *what do I need to do to get there?* Let's say for example you want to appear on a TED stage. You'll need a talk, a speaker sheet, a speaker page on your website, and a plan to get to the decision makers who will invite you to give that TED Talk.

Reverse engineer your success plan to build notoriety and credibility. Begin with a list of speaker goals: how much money will you be paid to speak, where will you speak, how frequently will you speak, and what will you speak on? Research the people who are already speaking at that level. What do their brands look like? Where do they contribute content, who endorses them, who follows them, and so on, and so on.

8. Make Rich Content Part of Your Plan

Your roadmap will be unique to you, your industry, your audience, and your personal goals—but the one thing that every successful roadmap has in common is rich content. All of your content matters; whether it's on your website, in an article you wrote, or in your marketing materials, content is king. Content is the only way to communicate your message, engage your audience, and get Google to rank you, and your website, as relevant.

Your website will be the home base for everything you do. The content on your website allows you to control the narrative of your brand and the actions of your readers. People will find you in a variety of ways, but they will, hopefully, all end up in the same place—your website.

Develop a content plan. It's okay to have a loose idea of what you will write about, and it's totally okay to introduce new concepts, but it's critical that you do this in a strategic and mindful way. Begin by developing a list of concepts that you will write about. Play with new concepts and pay attention to what resonates with your joy and your audience.

Plan on how you will release content and create a schedule to keep yourself on track. Recycled versions of your content will appear in myriad places on the internet as you contribute to blogs, periodicals, and books, as well as in social posts, comments, videos, podcasts, media interviews, and more. Every little thing you do counts; it bolsters your credibility and leads people back to your website. Speaking of, always ask for a link back to your website when you contribute content. Also, link out to mentions of you online and thank the influencers who helped you publish your works elsewhere. Link to those influencers, share their content, and they will do the same for you. This, my friends, is just the beginning of your visibility; it's the basis for your plan.

9. Make it Pretty

We have reached the part of the branding process that everyone expects to talk about—the visuals. Usually, the first thing people think about is the logo, but I'd like you to think beyond the logo. A successful brand is more than a logo—it's a signature color, a typeface, a style, an attitude; your brand needs a consistent look and feel that will appear on your website, business card, email signature, customized social media accounts, one-sheets, and more.

What's your look? How will people recognize you in every aspect of your brand? Are you edgy, soft, mysterious, professional, flippant, controversial, progressive, outrageous, cautious, or funny?

Keep in mind that the look you create needs to embody the feeling and tone of your voice; they support one another. From your logo and headshot to the way you dress, your products, your giveaways, and even your social media posts, everything you create needs to follow a set of style guides that you establish from the beginning.

A cohesive look will tie it all together. A polished and professional brand instills trust in your audience. If you take yourself seriously enough to create a polished brand, your audience will take you seriously too; they'll pay attention, and they will remember you and tell others about you. Bingo. Branding is about resonating on every level possible and continuing to resonate as often as possible.

10. Connect the Dots

All of your products and marketing collateral must support the brand. It's time to review your assets to see if they fit, or need an overhaul. Every piece in the chain must connect the dots of your brand. Each mention, product, piece of marketing collateral, talk, and appearance, and even your email signature, matters.

Check in often. This will be part of the plan. It's easy to put it off until later, but if later never comes, then your roadmap will fall apart. Think about it: when you take a road trip, you need to account for heavy traffic, construction, and roadblocks. If you plan ahead and check in, you can account for these minor inconveniences and adjust your plan. The same is true in business.

Tracking your ROI (return on investment) is the most obvious form of checking in, but there are so many little ways to check in that will help bolster that ROI. Things like following your audience engagement (what content attracts the most comments, shares, likes, and click-throughs) as well as tracking and understanding the impact of your website traffic are just as critical as knowing the number of book sales in a given month. What happened on the day you sold twice as many e-books as usual? Which article converted into a higher subscriber rate? What can you do to duplicate that success? How can you work that into your future plan?

You'll find that some of your efforts are ineffective. Knowing this allows you to adjust and spend your time more wisely. Time is perhaps the most precious part of your budget; you have a finite amount of time, and chasing your tail ensures chaos, not success.

I recommend that you set aside a specific day each week, or month, or quarter, and check in on the critical elements of your brand. You may decide to check in on some items more frequently, in order to stay connected to your plan.

Examples of Items to Include on Your Checklist

- **Website traffic:** learn how to effectively track your unique visitors, most popular- and unpopular-pages, bounce rate, and more, using Google analytics.
- **Content theme and website message:** does it still ring true?
- **Social engagement:** shares, likes, comments, click-throughs.
- **Blog categories:** are they in line with your brand mission and core values, do they offer value to your audience, do they bring you joy?
- **Posting calendar:** create an annual calendar to guide you in your content development and posting strategy. Track which posts get the most engagement and adjust your calendar as needed.
- **Website resources and tips:** add value to your content regularly, schedule new resources and tips quarterly so that your content does not grow stale.
- **Credibility:** add endorsements, testimonials, case studies, published works, speaker topics, and appearances to your bio and website often. Every little achievement must become part of the overall narrative.
- **Public profiles:** every time you create an online profile, track it in a spreadsheet, otherwise you might forget about it and it could turn into an anchor that holds you back.
- **Bio versions:** create several versions of your bio that you will use for different purposes, including a professional bio, a casual bio, a book jacket bio, a social media bio, a speaker bio, and a media bio. Track where these are posted and check in often to ensure that they don't get stale. Also, make sure to update them with your latest successes (impressive appearances, awards, associations, and more). Your bio is your introduction to your potential audience; make sure it represents you in the best way possible.

Begin!

Are you committed to you? It's time to stake your claim, establish your authority, build your online identity, and develop a personal style that is not only memorable, but also trustworthy. It's time to create a personal brand that will legitimize your presence in your industry and turn one-time readers into loyal followers.

Dream it. Believe it. Commit.

Commit to the daily grind. Commit to picking yourself up and starting over again, and again. Commit to the inevitable course correction that's needed to reach your goals, because no plan is ever perfect or static—just remember to keep your eye on your future success and you will get there. I promise.

You Are Worthy of Loyal Followers

My favorite side effect of a well-developed brand is the aphrodisiac of confidence building. A personal brand is the best confidence builder I've ever witnessed. As your message and your brand begin to take shape and "it" begins to feel real, you will feel a sense of validation and pride that is absolutely contagious.

Trust that you are worthy of speaking your truth, and trust that your truth is valuable and needed. Like all other skill sets, it's okay to take one step at a time. You are worthy of this time investment. Start small, but know you can grow your author power into a powerful, life-changing, earth-shaking brand.

Trust, my beautiful friend, trust.

ABOUT JENIFFER THOMPSON

Jeniffer Thompson is a personal branding expert, digital marketing strategist, and publishing consultant with more than twenty-years experience in the publishing industry. She is an author and speaker who delivers strategy-rich content and actionable tools that educate and empower authors. She is passionate about helping authors navigate their publishing choices and establish highly visible author brands that sell books. Mrs. Thompson is a co-founder of the San Diego Writers Festival; she serves on the boards of Publishers and Writers of San Diego, and the San Diego Memoir Writers Association. She is also the founder and principal at Monkey C Media, an award-winning design firm specializing in book packaging, author websites, and digital marketing strategies. Follow her blog at JenifferThompson.com, and visit her company website at monkeyCmedia.com.

CONNECT WITH JENIFFER

Visit her at
MonkeyCMedia.com

Get your FREE eBook:

*How to Write a Professional Bio
for Authors and Thought Leaders*

when you subscribe to her blog at JenifferThompson.com

Facebook
facebook.com/JenifferThompsonConsulting

Instagram
Instagram.com/jeniffer_grace

LinkedIn
Linkedin.com/in/jenifferthompson

RESOURCES

Writing Associations/Groups/Organizations /Online Sites

- The Authors Guild: www.authorsguild.org
- The International Women's Writing Guild: www.iwwg.org
- American Society of Journalists and Authors: www.asja.org
- Association of Writers & Writing Programs: www.awpwriter.org
- Nonfiction Authors Association: www.nonfictionauthorsassociation.com
- National Writers Union: www.nwu.org
- Pen America: www.pen.org
- Women's National Book Association: www.wnba-books.org
- Poets & Writers: www.pw.org
- Writers Guild of America West: www.wga.org
- San Diego Memoir Writers Association: www.sdmwa.org
- Thought Leaders Who Write – Facebook Group: www.facebook.com/thoughtleaderswhowrite
- The Feisty Writer: www.thefeistywriter.com

Books on Writing

- *7 Essential Writing Tools: That Will Absolutely Make Your Writing Better (And Enliven Your Soul)* by Marni Freedman
- *The Business of Being a Writer (Chicago Guides to Writing, Editing, and Publishing)* by Jane Friedman
- *Haiku Mind: 108 Poems to Cultivate Awareness & Open Your Heart* by Patricia Donegan
- *The Heart of Haiku* by Jane Hirshfield

- *The Chicago Manual of Style: The Essential Guide for Writers, Editors, and Publishers* by the University of Chicago Press
- *Wild Women, Wild Voices: Writing From Your Authentic Wildness* by Judy Reeves
- *The Comic Toolbox: How to Be Funny Even If You're Not* by John Vorhaus
- *Bird by Bird: Some Instructions on Writing and Life* by Anne Lamott
- *On Writing Well: The Classic Guide to Writing Nonfiction* by William Zinsser
- *On Writing: A Memoir of the Craft* by Stephen King (King shares inspiring advice, helpful tips, and personal experiences about his life as a writer.)
- *The Elements of Style* by William Strunk Jr. and E.B. White
- *The Artist's Way: A Spiritual Path to Higher Creativity* by Julia Cameron

Note About the Vignettes

Though the vignettes are based on real people and events, at times identifying factors such as names, descriptions, and subject matter have been changed to protect the identity of either the person or the project, or both.

Note on Abraham Maslow's Hierarchy of Needs

Abraham Maslow (1908-1970): American psychologist who, after studying the needs of human beings, created a theory of psychological health known as "Maslow's Hierarchy of Needs." To learn more about Maslow's Hierarchy of Needs, see "A Theory of Human Motivation," Maslow's original article published in 1943.

Notes on the Tell 'Em Method of Communication

"Tell 'em what you're going to tell 'em. Tell 'em.
Tell 'em what you told 'em."

This advice has been attributed to many thinkers, including Aristotle, Dale Carnegie, J. H. Jowett, Fred E. Marble, Royal Meeker, Henry Koster, and Paul White.

NOTABLE BOOKS OR ESSAYS FROM EARLY FEMALE THOUGHT LEADERS

Author's note: This is not a complete or exhaustive list. This list is meant to introduce you to some of the women who have been using the power of their words to impact their corner of the world.

(Listed by date.)

The Book of the City of Ladies or *Le Livre de la Cité des Dames* by Christine de Pizan, translated by Rosalind Brown-Grant (finished by 1405)

Le Promenoir de M. de Montaigne qui traite de l'amour dans l'œuvre de Plutarque by Marie le Jars de Gournay (1584)

Grief des dames by Marie Le Jars de Gournay (1626), translated into English as *The Ladies' Grievance*

A Serious Proposal to the Ladies, for the Advancement of Their True and Greatest Interest by Mary Astell (1694)

A Vindication of the Rights of Woman by Mary Wollstonecraft (1790)

"An Address to the Public; Particularly to the Members of the Legislature of New York, Proposing a Plan for Improving Female Education" by Emma Willard (1819)

"The Times that Try Men's Souls" by Maria Weston Chapman (1837)

"Voting Rights Speech" by Elizabeth Cady Stanton (1848)

"Declaration of Sentiments and Resolutions" by Elizabeth Cady Stanton et al. (1848)

"Ain't I a Woman?" by Sojourner Truth (1851)

Incidents in the Life of a Slave Girl by Harriet Jacobs (1861)

Behind the Scenes: Or, Thirty Years a Slave and Four Years in the White House by Elizabeth Keckley (1868)

Woman's Rights to the Suffrage by Susan B. Anthony (1872)

Narrative of Sojourner Truth by Sojourner Truth and Nell Irvin Painter (1884)

Eighty Years and More; Reminiscences 1815–1897 by Elizabeth Cady Stanton (1897)

The Light of Truth: Writings of an Anti-Lynching Crusader by Ida B. Wells (late 19th century)

American Indian Stories, Legends, and Other Writings by Zitkala-Sa (1910)

Marriage and Love by Emma Goldman (1911)

"Freedom or Death" by Emmeline Pankhurst (1913)

A Room of One's Own by Virginia Woolf (1929)

The Suffragette Movement: An Intimate Account of Persons and Ideals by E. Sylvia Pankhurst (1931)

The Diary of a Young Girl by Anne Frank (1942-1944)

Woman as Force in History. A Study in Traditions and Realities by Mary Ritter Beard (1946)

The Second Sex by Simone de Beauvoir (1949)

The Myth of Women's Inferiority by Evelyn Reed (1954)

Unshackled: The Story of How We Won the Vote by Christabel Pankhurst (1959)

The Feminine Mystique by Betty Friedan (1963)

"A Bunny's Tale, Part I & II" by Gloria Steinem (1963)

The Bell Jar by Sylvia Plath (1963)

I Know Why the Caged Bird Sings by Maya Angelou (1969)

"Equal Rights for Women" by Shirley Chisholm (1969)

Sexual Politics by Kate Millett (1970)

Fear *of Flying* by Erica Jong (1973)

Our Bodies, Ourselves by The Boston Women's Health Book Collective (1973)

"Fat is A Feminist Issue" by Susie Orbach (1978)

Ain't I a Woman: Black Women and Feminism by Bell Hooks (1981)

Women, Race & Class by Angela Y. Davis (1983)

Outrageous Acts and Everyday Rebellions by Gloria Steinem (1983)

In Search of Our Mothers' Gardens: Womanist Prose by Alice Walker (1983)

Sister Outsider: Essays and Speeches by Audre Lorde (1984)

Ice & Fire by Andrea Dworkin (1986)

If Women Counted: A New Feminist Economics by Marilyn Waring (1988)

The Beauty Myth: How Images of Beauty Are Used Against Women by Naomi Wolf (1990)

Women Who Run With the Wolves: Myths and Stories of the Wild Woman Archetype by Clarissa Pinkola Estés, PhD (1992)

BOOKS MENTIONED IN *PERMISSION TO ROAR*

A

Dear Ijeawele, or a Feminist Manifesto in Fifteen Suggestions by Chimamanda Ngozi Adichie

We Should All Be Feminists by Chimamanda Ngozi Adichie

The New Jim Crow: Mass Incarcerations in the Age of Colorblindness by Michelle Alexander

Chocolate for a Teen's Soul: Life-Changing Stories for Young Women About Growing Wise and Growing Strong by Kay Allenbaugh

#GIRLBOSS by Sophia Amoruso

And Still I Rise: A Book of Poems by Maya Angelou

I Know Why the Caged Bird Sings by Maya Angelou

12 Steps to a Compassionate Life by Karen Armstrong

The Origins of Totalitarianism by Hannah Arendt

A History of God: The 4,000-Year Quest of Judaism, Christianity and Islam by Karen Armstrong

The Highly Sensitive Person: How to Thrive When the World Overwhelms You by Elaine N. Aron, PhD

This Won't Hurt a Bit (And Other White Lies): My Education in Medicine and Motherhood by Michelle Au

B

The Brain Boost Diet Plan: 4 Weeks To Optimize Your Mood, Memory and Brain Health for Life by Christine Bailey

How Remarkable Women Lead: The Breakthrough Model for Work and Life by Joanna Barsh and Susie Cranston

Simple Abundance: A Daybook of Comfort and Joy by Sarah Ban Breathnach

Women & Power: A Manifesto by Mary Beard

Codependent No More: How to Stop Controlling Others and Start Caring for Yourself by Melody Beattie

Finding Your Own North Star: Claiming the Life You Were Meant to Live by Martha Beck

The Joy Diet: 10 Daily Practices for a Happier Life by Martha Beck

May Cause Miracles: A 40-Day Guidebook of Subtle Shifts for Radical Change and Unlimited Happiness by Gabrielle Bernstein

The Universe Has Your Back: Transform Fear to Faith by Gabrielle Bernstein

Jesus Feminist: An Invitation to Revisit the Bible's View of Women by Sarah Bessey and Rachel Held Evans

Memories in Dragonflies: Simple Lessons for Mindful Dying by Lannette Cornell Bloom

In the Company of Women: Inspiration and Advice From over 100 Makers, Artists, and Entrepreneur by Grace Bonney

The Writers Market: The Most Trusted Guide to Getting Published edited by Robert Lee Brewer

The Money Therapist: A Woman's Guide to Creating A Healthy Financial Life by Marcia Brixey

Ready to Be a Thought Leader? How to Increase Your Influence, Impact, and Success by Denise Brosseau

Daring Greatly: How the Courage to Be Vulnerable Transforms the Way We Live, Love, Parent, and Lead by Brené Brown

The Gifts of Imperfection: Let Go of Who You Think You're Supposed to Be and Embrace Who You Are by Brené Brown

I Thought It Was Just Me (But It Isn't): Making the Journey From "What Will People Think?" to "I Am Enough" by Brené Brown

Knowing Your Value: Women, Money and Getting What You're Worth by Mika Brzezinski

C

80 Years and More: Reminiscences 1815-1897 by Elizabeth Cady Stanton

Quiet: The Power of Introverts in a World That Can't Stop Talking by Susan Cain

The Artist's Way: A Spiritual Path to Higher Creativity by Julia Cameron

It's Never Too Late to Begin Again: Discovering Creativity and Meaning at Midlife and Beyond by Julia Cameron with Emma Lively

Chicken Soup for the Teenage Soul: 101 Stories of Life, Love and Learning by Jack Canfield, Mark Victor Hansen, and Kimberly Kirberger

Silent Spring by Rachel Carson

Rage Becomes Her: The Power of Women's Anger by Soraya Chemaly

The 10-Day Green Smoothie Cleanse: Lose 10 Pounds of Stubborn Body Fat in 7 Days by Valerie Childs

When Things Fall Apart: Heart Advice for Difficult Times by Pema Chodron

Woman Hollering Creek and Other Stories by Sandra Cisneros

Leave Me Alone, I'm Reading: Finding and Losing Myself in Books by Maureen Corrigan

A Woman's Way Through The 12 Steps by Stephanie S. Covington

Presence: Bringing your BOLDEST SELF to your BIGGEST Challenges by Amy Cuddy

Storm in a Teacup: The Physics of Everyday Life by Helen Czerski

D

The Second Sex by Simone de Beauvoir

It's Okay That You're Not Okay: Meeting Grief and Loss in a Culture that Doesn't Understand by Megan Devine and Mark Nepo

Slouching Towards Bethlehem: Essays by Joan Didion

100 Days to Brave by Annie F. Downs

Love Warrior by Glennon Doyle

Carry On, Warrior: The Power of Embracing Your Messy, Beautiful Life by Glennon Doyle Melton

Devotions From the Garden: Finding Peace and Rest in Your Hurried Life by Miriam Drennan

Grit by Angela Duckworth.

E

The Vagina Monologues by Eve Ensler

I Feel Bad About My Neck: And Other Thoughts on Being a Woman by Nora Ephron

Women Who Run With the Wolves: Myths and Stories of the Wild Woman Archetype by Clarissa Pinkola Estés, PhD

F

Good Night Stories for Rebel Girls by Elena Favilli and Francesca Cavallo

No Excuses: Nine Ways Women Can Change How We Think About Power by Gloria Feldt

The Freedom Writers Diary: How a Teacher and 150 Teens Used Writing to Change Themselves and the World Around Them by Zlata Filipovic

Five Days at Memorial: Life and Death in a Storm-Ravaged Hospital by Sheri Fink

Overcoming Fear, Worry, and Anxiety: Becoming a Woman of Faith and Confidence by Elyse Fitzpatrick

Break Your Own Rules: How to Change the Patterns of Thinking that Block Women's Paths to Power by Jill Flynn and Kathryn Heath

Nice Girls Don't Get the Corner Office: Unconscious Mistakes Women Make That Sabotage Their Careers (A NICE GIRLS Book) by Lois P. Frankel

Girl Positive: How Girls Are Shaping a New World by Tatiana Fraser and Caia Hagel

The 10-Day Plan to Nourish and Glow: Lose Weight, Feel Great, and Transform Your Relationship with Food by Amelia Freer

The Feminine Mystique by Betty Friedan

The Business of Being a Writer by Jane Friedman

G

The Path of Transformation: How Healing Ourselves Can Change the World by Shakti Gawain

Bad Feminist: Essays by Roxane Gay

Not That Bad: Dispatches From Rape Culture edited by Roxane Gay

Big Magic: Creative Living Beyond Fear by Elizabeth Gilbert

Before the Change: Taking Charge of Your Perimenopause by Ann Louise Gittleman, PhD.

The New Fat Flush Plan: The Breakthrough Detox Diet by Ann Louise Gittleman, PhD. C.N.S.

8 Steps to a Pain-Free Back: Remember When it Didn't Hurt by Esther Gokhale, L.Ac. with Susan Adams

Never Threaten to Eat Your Co-Workers: Best of Blogs edited by Alan Graham and Bonnie Burton

H

Are You There, Vodka? It's Me, Chelsea by Chelsea Handler

Sister Citizen: Shame, Stereotypes, and Black Women in America by Melissa V. Harris-Perry

The Myth of the Nice Girl: Achieving a Career You Love Without Becoming a Person You Hate by Fran Hauser

Empowering Women: Every Woman's Guide to Successful Living by Louise Hay

You Can Heal Your Life by Louise Hay

Women Who Worry Too Much: How to Stop Worry and Anxiety From Ruining Relationships, Work and Fun by Holly Hazlett-Stevens

Hardball for Women: Winning at the Game of Business by Pat Heim, Tammy Hughes, and Susan K. Golant

Chicken Soup for the Soul: Devotional Stories for Women; 101 Daily Devotions to Comfort, Encourage, and Inspire Women by Susan M. Heim & Karen C. Talcott

How Women Rise: Break the 12 Habits Holding You Back From Your Next Raise, Promotion, or Job by Sally Helgesen and Michael Goldsmith

Healing After Loss: Daily Meditations for Working Through Grief by Martha W. Hickman

Clean Eating: 151 Healthy and Delicious Recipes for Eating Clean by Susan Hollister

Ain't I a Woman? Black Women and Feminism by Bell Hooks

Feminism Is for Everybody: Passionate Politics by Bell Hooks

The Not So Subtle Art of Being a Fat Girl: Loving the Skin You're In by Tess Holliday

Thrive: The Third Metric to Redefining Success and Creating a Life of Well-Being, Wisdom, and Wonder by Arianna Huffington

J

Sugar Crush: How to Reduce Inflammation, Reverse Nerve Damage, and Reclaim Good Health by Dr. Richard P. Jacoby and Raquel Baldelomar

Women, Food, and Desire: Honor Your Cravings, Embrace Your Desires, Reclaim Your Body by Alexandra Jamieson

This Will Be My Undoing: Living at the Intersection of Black, Female, and Feminist in (White) America by Morgan Jenkins

Mad Woman on the Loose by Marael Johnson

Fear of Flying by Erica Jong

K

Loving What Is: Four Questions That Can Change Your Life by Byron Katie

Diary of a Mad Housewife: A Novel by Sue Kaufman

APE: Author, Publisher, Entrepreneur—How to Publish a Book by Guy Kawasaki and Shawn Welch

The Confidence Code: The Science and Art of Self-Assurance—What Women Should Know by Katty Kay & Claire Shipman

Girl, Interrupted by Susanna Kaysen

The Woman Warrior: Memoirs of Girlhood Among Ghosts by Maxine Hong Kingston

No Logo by Naomi Klein

Appetites: Why Women Want by Caroline Knapp

*You Do You: How to Be Who You Are and Use What You've Got to Get What You Want (A No F*cks Given Guide)* by Sarah Knight

The Sixth Extinction: An Unnatural History by Elizabeth Kolbert

The Life-Changing Magic of Tidying Up: The Japanese Art of Decluttering and Organizing by Marie Kondo

One Day We'll All Be Dead and None of This Will Matter: Essays by Scaachi Koul

On Life After Death by Elisabeth Kübler-Ross

L

Bird by Bird: Some Instructions on Writing and Life by Anne Lamott

Help, Thanks, Wow: The Three Essential Prayers by Anne Lamott

Women Rocking Business: The Ultimate Step-by-Step Guidebook to Create a Thriving Life Doing Work You Love by Sage Lavine

100 Days of Real Food: How We Did It, What We Learned, and 100 Easy, Wholesome Recipes Your Family Will Love by Lisa Leake

Broken Open: How Difficult Times Can Help Us Grow by Elizabeth Lesser

Guerrilla Marketing for Writers: 100 No-Cost, Low Cost Weapons for Selling Your Work by Jay Conrad Levinson and Rick Frishman

Gift From the Sea by Anne Morrow Lindbergh

Sister Outsider: Essays and Speeches by Audre Lorde

M

The Earth, My Butt and Other Big Round Things by Carolyn Mackler

The Conquer Kit: A Creative Business Planner for Women Entrepreneurs by Natalie MacNeil

Household Education by Harriet Martineau

A Year Full of Stories: 52 Folk Tales and Legends From Around the World by Angela McAllister and Christopher Corr

More: Journey to Mystical Union Through the Sacred and the Profane by Mariah McKenzie

I Choose Me (Every Day & Always) by Danielle Leduc McQueen

This Close to Happy: A Reckoning with Depression by Daphne Merkin

Unlimited: A Three-Step Plan For Achieving Your Dreams by Jillian Michaels

Playing Big: Practical Wisdom for Women Who Want to Speak Up, Create, and Lead by Tara Mohr

So Long, Insecurity: You've Been a Bad Friend to Us by Beth Moore

A Good Time to Be a Girl: Don't Lean In, Change the System by Helena Morrissey

Sacred Contracts: Awakening Your Divine Potential by Carolyn Myss

N

Reading Lolita in Tehran: A Memoir in Books by Azar Nafisi

Chicken Soup for the Soul: The Empowered Woman; 101 Stories about Being Confident, Courageous and Your True Self by Amy Newmark

O

Flying Lessons and Other Stories edited by Ellen Oh

So You Want to Talk About Race by Ljeoma Oluo

Girls and Sex: Navigating the Complicated New Landscape by Peggy Orenstein

The Road to Wealth: The Answers You Need to More Than 2,000 Personal Financial Questions by Suze Orman

No Mexicans, Women, or Dogs Allowed: The Rise of the Mexican American Civil Rights Movement by Cynthia E. Orozco

P

Free Women, Free Men: Sex, Gender, Feminism by Camille Paglia

Dear Madam President: An Open Letter to the Women Who Will Run the World by Jennifer Palmieri

The 10-Day Belly Slim Down: Lose Your Belly, Heal Your Gut, Enjoy a Lighter, Younger You by Kellyann Petrucci MS ND

Let it Shine: Stories of Black Women Freedom Fighters by Andrea Davis Pinkney

Power Through Partnership: How Women Lead Better Together by Betsy Polk and Maggie Ellis Chotas

The Fast Metabolism Diet: Eat More Food and Lose More Weight by Haylie Pomroy

How To Break Up With Your Phone: The 30-Day Plan to Take Back Your Life by Catherine Price

R

Dark Matter and the Dinosaurs: The Astounding Interconnectedness of the Universe by Lisa Randall

The Metabolism Plan: Discover the Foods and Exercises that Work for Your Body to Reduce Inflammation and Drop Pounds Fast by Lyn-Genet Recitas

Wild Women, Wild Voices: Writing From Your Authentic Wildness by Judy Reeves

Kitchen Table Wisdom: Stories That Heal by Rachel Naomi Remen, MD

Year of Yes: How to Dance It Out, Stand in the Sun and Be Your Own Person by Shonda Rhimes

Make Trouble: Standing Up, Speaking Out, and Finding the Courage to Lead by Cecile Richards

Stop Dressing Your Six-Year-Old Like as Skank: A Slightly Tarnished Southern Belle's Words of Wisdom by Celia Rivenbark

Selling Anxiety: How the News Media Scare Women by Caryl Rivers

Bonk: The Curious Coupling of Science and Sex by Mary Roach

Breaking Free From Emotional Eating by Geneen Roth

This Messy Magnificent Life: A Field Guide by Geneen Roth

The Four Tendencies: The Indispensable Personality Profiles That Reveal How to Make Your Life Better (and other People's Lives Better, Too) by Gretchen Rubin

The Happiness Project: Or, Why I Spent a Year Trying to Sing in the Morning, Clean My Closets, Fight Right, Read Aristotle, and Generally Have More Fun by Gretchen Rubin

S

Hospital: Man, Woman, Birth, Death, Infinity, Plus Red Tape, Bad Behavior, Money, God, and Diversity on Steroids by Julie Salamon

Even God Is Single (So Stop Giving Me a Hard Time): The Book Every Single Girl Needs to Defend Against Nudgy Family and Friends by Karen Salmansohn

Create Your Writer Platform: The Key to Building an Audience, Selling More Books, and Finding Success as an Author by Chuck Sambuchino

Lean In: Women, Work, and the Will to Lead by Sheryl Sandberg

Option B: Facing Adversity, Building Resilience, and Finding Joy by Sheryl Sandberg and Adam Grant

Change Your Life Without Getting Out of Bed: The Ultimate Nap Book by Sark

Eat Mangoes Naked: Finding Pleasure Everywhere (and Dancing with the Pits) by Sark

Living Juicy: Daily Morsels for Your Creative Soul by Sark

The Emotionally Healthy Woman: Eight Things You Have to Quit to Change Your Life by Geri Scazzero with Peter Scazzero

Women, Spirituality and Transformative Leadership: Where Grace Meets Power edited by Kathe Schaaf, Kay Lindahl, Kathleen S. Purty, PhD, and Reverend Guo Cheen

I Still Miss My Man: But My Aim Is Getting Better by Sarah Shankman

Hidden Figures: The American Dream and the Untold Story of the Black Women Mathematicians Who Helped Win the Space Race by Margot Lee Shetterly

You Are a Badass: How to Stop Doubting Your Greatness and Start Living an Awesome Life by Jen Sincero

How to Be a Bawse: A Guide to Conquering Life by Lilly Singh

Women Who Dared: 52 Stories of Fearless Daredevils, Adventurers and Rebels by Linda Skeers

Unfinished Business: Women, Men, Work, Family by Anne-Marie Slaughter

10-Day Green Smoothie Cleanse by JJ Smith

The Glass Universe: How the Ladies of the Harvard Observatory Took the Measure of the Stars by Dava Sobel

Men Explain Things To Me by Rebecca Solnit

Working with Difficult People by Muriel Solomon

Against Interpretation and Other Essays by Susan Sontag

Secrets of Six-Figure Women: Surprising Strategies to Up Your Earnings and Change Your Life by Barbara Stanny

Outrageous Acts and Everyday Rebellions by Gloria Steinem

Wild: From Lost to Found on the Pacific Crest Trail by Cheryl Strayed

T

My Stroke of Insight: A Brain Scientist's Personal Journey by Jill Bolte Taylor

Girls Think of Everything: Stories of Ingenious Inventions by Women by Catherine Thimmesh

I Don't Wait Anymore: Letting Go of Expectations and Grasping God's Adventure for You by Grace Thornton

Narrative of Sojourner Truth by Sojourner Truth

U

Well-Behaved Women Seldom Make History by Laurel Thatcher Ulrich

We're Going to Need More Wine: Stories by Gabrielle Union

V

Eating Clean: The 21-Day Plan to Detox, Fight Inflammation, and Reset Your Body by Amie Valpone

The Body Keeps the Score: Brain, Mind, and Body in the Healing of Trauma by Bessel van der Kolk, MD

Women in Tech: Take Your Career to the Next Level With Practical Advice and Inspiring Stories by Tarah Wheeler Van Vlack

One Day My Soul Just Opened Up: 40 Days and 40 Nights Toward Spiritual Strength and Personal Growth by Iyanla Vanzant

W

In Search of Our Mothers' Gardens: Womanist Prose by Alice Walker

The Glass Castle: A Memoir by Jeannette Walls

How to Have a Good Day: Harness the Power of Behavioral Science to Transform Your Working Life by Caroline Webb

Shrill: Notes From a Loud Woman by Lindy West

Educated: A Memoir by Tara Westover

I Shouldn't Be Telling You This: How to Ask for the Money, Snag the Promotion, and Create the Career You Deserve by Kate White

Sippy Cups Are Not for Chardonnay: And Other Things I Had to Learn as a New Mom by Stephanie Wilder-Taylor

A Return to Love: Reflections on the Principles of a Course in Miracles by Marianne Williamson

A Woman's Worth by Marianne Williamson

The Wisdom of Sundays: Life-Changing Insights From Super Soul Conversations by Oprah Winfrey

How Women Mean Business: A Step by Step Guide to Profiting From Gender Balanced Business by Avivah Wittenberg-Cox

The Beauty Myth: How Images of Beauty Are Used Against Women by Naomi Wolf

The Pre-Diabetes Diet Plan: How to Reverse Prediabetes and Prevent Diabetes through Healthy Eating and Exercise by Hillary Wright

BOOK CLUB RESOURCES

For a "Thought Leaders Who Write" Book Club – Marni's Top 20 Favorites

1. *Daring Greatly: How the Courage to Be Vulnerable Transforms the Way We Live, Love, Parent, and Lead* by Brené Brown
2. *The Artist's Way* by Julia Cameron
3. *Good Night Stories for Rebel Girls* by Elena Favilli and Francesca Cavallo
4. *When Things Fall Apart: Heart Advice for Difficult Times* by Pema Chodron
5. *Grit* by Angela Duckworth
6. *Women Who Run With the Wolves* by Clarissa Pinkola Estés
7. *Help, Thanks, Wow: The Three Essential Prayers* by Anne Lamott
8. *Sacred Contracts: Awakening Your Divine Potential* by Carolyn Myss
9. *I Know Why the Caged Bird Sings* by Maya Angelou
10. *This Messy Magnificent Life: A Field Guide* by Geneen Roth
11. *Big Magic: Creative Living Beyond Fear* by Elizabeth Gilbert
12. *Women Rocking Business: The Ultimate Step-by-Step Guidebook to Create a Thriving Life Doing Work You Love* by Sage Levine
13. *Living Juicy: Daily Morsels for Your Creative Soul* by Sark
14. *Men Explain Things To Me* by Rebecca Solnit
15. *May Cause Miracles: A 40-Day Guidebook of Subtle Shifts for Radical Change and Unlimited Happiness* by Gabrielle Bernstein
16. *Outrageous Acts and Everyday Rebellions* by Gloria Steinem
17. *The Body Keeps the Score: Brain, Mind, and Body in the Healing of Trauma* by Bessel van der Kolk, MD

18. *A Return to Love: Reflections on the Principles of a Course in Miracles* by Marianne Williamson
19. *Year of Yes: How to Dance It Out, Stand in the Sun and Be Your Own Person* by Shonda Rhimes
20. *Loving What Is: Four Questions That Can Change Your Life* by Byron Katie

How to Create a Thought Leader Book Club

Decide on a place to meet monthly. Choose three or four books in advance so everyone can order them. Make the atmosphere comfortable and celebratory. Be supportive of all opinions. Minimize cross-talk. Bring food from time to time. Bring wine from time to time. Put older and newer books on the list. Encourage new members to join.

Book Club Questions

1. What inspired you to purchase/read this book?
2. What need was this book speaking to?
3. What was the promise of the book?
4. Did the book fulfill its promise?
5. If you had one critique about the book, what would it be?
6. How did the author use her authentic writer's voice?
7. Did you feel a sense of kinship with the author?
8. Did you learn new information?
9. What was your biggest takeaway after reading the book? If you could ask the author one question, what would it be?

ACKNOWLEDGMENTS

I would like to thank my editors, Tracy J. Jones, Carlos de los Rios, and Erin Willard.

I would like to thank my mom, Natalie, my husband, Carlos, my son, Ben, and my best friend in the whole world, Tracy, for being my constant, ongoing cheerleaders. I would also like to thank my cats, Mr. Beef and Dorothy J. Witten for staying up with me late at night as I struggled to meet deadlines for the book. I would like to thank my wonderful Thursday writing group, The Feisty Writers, and the greatest writing tribe:

Tracy J. Jones	Lois Sunrich	Justin Hudnall
Jeniffer Thompson	Elise Capron	Alexa Grossman
Marijke McCandles	KamalaDevi McClure	Jordan Grossman
Elizabeth Oppen Eshoo	Brian Joyner	Evan Grossman
Anastasia Zadeik	Dan Amato	Annie Leake
Lindsey Salatka	Jennifer Coburn	Edythe Wexler
Suzanne Spector	Marlo Thomas	Allan Musterer
Anna Menniti	Franciene Lehmann	Lori Mitchell
Nancy G. Villalobos	Michelle Goane	Laura Engel
Donna Brown Agins	John Vorhaus	Kathy Pease
Andrea Moser	Judy A. Bernstein	Alyssa Walters
Kimberly Joy	Danielle B. Baldwin	Marisa Luque
Phyllis Olins	Shawna Rawlinson	Phil Johnson
Karen Laugesen Russell	Vincentia Schroeter	Jill G. Hall
KM McNeel	Rick Bollinger	Judy Reeves
Jen Laffler	John Cunningham	Brooke Warner
Mahshid Hager	Lucy Rose	Andrea Moriarty
Kristen Fogle	Jennifer Gasner	Gina Simmons
Susan Keith	Cherie Kephart	Sher Kreiger
Lynn Cooper	Jazmine Gelfand	UCSD
Shiloh Rasmussen	Nicola Ranson	San Diego Writers, Ink
Barbara Thomson	Nicole Weiss	The San Diego
Caroline Gilman	Bethel Swift	Public Library System
Madonna Treadway	Susan McBeth	

37658226R00199

Made in the USA
Middletown, DE
01 March 2019